Contributors:
Simon Allaby . Doug Barne...
Stuart Bell . Ray Bevan
Gavin Collins . Mark Conner
Anthony Delaney . Terry Eckersley
David Hall . Greg Haslam
Graham James . J.John
Simon McIntyre . Allan Meyer
Nigel Mumford . Rich Nathan
Ed Olsworth-Peter . Mary Pytches
Michael Rees . Rob Richards
John Ryeland . Tim Saiet
David Shearman . Roger Simpson
Jill Sweetman . Ruth Turner
Simon Vibert

PROCLAIMING MARRIAGE

27 timeless talks and sermons
Edited by **J.John**

Published in the UK by Philo Trust

Copyright © 2014 J.John

Published 2014 by Philo Trust, Witton House, Lower Road, Chorleywood,
Rickmansworth, WD3 5LB, United Kingdom

www.philotrust.com

The right of J.John to be identified as the Editor of this Work has been asserted by
him in accordance with the Copyright, Designs and Patents Act 1988.

British Library Cataloguing in Publication Data

A catalogue record for this book is available from the British Library

ISBN: 978-0-9928399-3-2

Design by Rachel Fung

Typeset by Verité CM Ltd

Printed and bound in the UK

CONTENTS

PREFACE
J.John

There are very few functions that are as complex, tension-packed and demanding as the modern wedding. You need a bride, groom, best man, wedding ring, bridesmaids, flowers, photographers, caterers, cars, music and a dozen other things and they all have to come together neatly without losing Aunt Daisy, the kids getting at the wine or war breaking out between family members. And if it's any sort of Christian wedding then, in the middle of this precision-timed, minutely scrutinised and precisely choreographed succession of ritual, rejoicing and refreshments, someone – normally a minister – stands up to give a few words about what marriage means.

In my experience wedding talks are – as befits the importance of the occasion – prepared with thought, effort and prayer. If they are done properly – and most are (although I have heard some bad ones!) – then they have something very serious and important to say because marriage is both serious and important. Unfortunately, whatever their wisdom and relevance, they are frequently, and undeservedly, overlooked. There is too much else going on in a marriage service for it to be the place for attentive and reflective listening. There are too many other emotions. Some of the congregation are simply relieved, either that they made it, that the bride really did turn up or that no one else is wearing the same outfit as them. Others are desperately trying to remember who the woman with the pink hat is and who Uncle Charlie is married to now. Still others are reflecting on the success or failure of their own relationships. Anyone involved in organising the ceremony is probably either too exhausted or too traumatised for the words to sink in. And those to whom these words are primarily addressed – the bride and groom – are doubtless preoccupied with their own joys, nerves and fears. In short, wedding addresses like these do not get the audience they deserve.

It is precisely because they do deserve an audience that I have collected these twenty-seven very different talks. We have collected these talks for ministers to see how others speak and preach at weddings and for married couples to marinade in timeless principles. For all of us who are concerned about marriage – and we all should be – they merit reading and thinking over. There's a wide range of wisdom in them, but let me suggest that they make four very important points about marriage, all of which we need to hear.

The first point made in these pages is the need for marriage to be *clarified*. These are confusing times and confusion is often contagious. Nowhere is this confusion more abundant than in the area of marriage, an institution that has unfortunately found itself on the frontline of the 'culture war' between the traditional Christian view and the post-Christian outlook on life that increasingly dominates our culture. On the subject of what marriage is all about, the church and the world say very different things. If you have no belief in God, then a wedding today is presumably little more than a formal public (and rather expensive) way of expressing the intensity of your love for someone else. While Christians would sympathise with the idea of a public expression of love, we believe that a wedding has a much richer, deeper and more sacred significance. For us, marriage is a serious and binding institution between a man and a woman, given by the God who made us, loves us and who has redeemed us in Jesus Christ. Marriage is an area where we need to do some clear thinking and these talks will help us to do just that.

The second point that these addresses make clear is that marriage should be *celebrated*. I said that marriage is serious and important – and it is – but we must never forget that it is a very good thing and a wedding is something that should be the subject of a wonderful and triumphant joy. Love and marriage are gifts of God and are things to be gloried in. It is worth remembering that when the Bible looks forward to the end of history and a new universe without evil, it unashamedly talks about it being 'the wedding of the Lamb' (Revelation 19:6–9). At weddings and in the marriages, there is something of heaven. You may say that this is hardly a Christian distinctive, because everybody celebrates at weddings. Yet despite the fact that there is a lot of jollity and fun at weddings, if you observe carefully you will detect that the note of celebration is sometimes thin and brittle. There is increasingly a cynical, even bitter, attitude to weddings. Examine any collection of jokes and sayings on marriage and you will find that almost all are sarcastic. So if, as Simon Allaby points out in his talk, marriage is a matter of 'give and take', many people today view it as *mis*givings and *mis*takes. And there are numerous weary jokes on the fact that those two little words 'I do' make up the 'longest sentence' in the English language. Of course, there are facts behind the bitterness: the odds are not good for the success of a marriage. (The current statistics are that 42 per cent of marriages in England and Wales end in divorce.) The result is an unspoken assumption that the promises made are probably not going to be kept and that today's joyful union is going to become tomorrow's war zone. So we need to be reminded that a wedding is an extraordinary, joyful and special event that should be celebrated with joy. In these talks, you will find that great note of celebration.

The third point emphasised here is that marriage should be *cherished*. The New Testament is blunt about this: 'Marriage should be honoured by all, and the marriage bed kept pure, for God will judge the adulterer and all the sexually immoral' (Hebrews 13:4). There are so many alternative ways of 'living together' today that marriage is no longer the pivotal, unique, once-in-a-lifetime event that it used to be. Yet despite all the alternatives, marriage is important and we need to recognise that fact. Marriage is important for society. Yes, it has its noisy critics but most people would agree that marriage is the foundation of a stable family and a stable society. To say this is not of course to be negative about singleness or even single parenting; it is, however, to make the point that the idea and value of marriage should be something that we honour and cherish. Without the standard of marriage, a society dissolves into a series of fluid, ever-changing relationships in which people, especially children, are damaged. Marriage is also important for individuals. Marriage should be the place where our wounds are healed and our gifts for life are developed. We all have bad and good features in our personality and in marriage a spouse can help their partner supress their worst and express their best. As the cynics point out, a marriage may be the closest thing to hell on earth. Nevertheless, it can also be the closest thing to heaven. We all need to value and cherish marriage.

The final point made repeatedly in these pages is the fact that marriage needs to be *championed*. Marriage has always had its opponents and never more so than at present. We need to stick up for marriage as an institution and there is much here that does this. Yet we also need to stick up for the individuals in marriage. To believe in marriage in the Christian sense and to commit to one another, in the words of the traditional wedding service 'for better for worse, for richer for poorer, in sickness and in health', is to choose to swim against a very strong current. As these talks point out, to do this is far from easy. There is a curiosity here that needs exposing. Today's atheists deride Christians for our naive lack of realism in believing what we do about God. Yet when it comes to marriage, it is obvious that it is they who are the fantasists ('all you need is love') and we who are the hard-headed realists. The reality is that maintaining a lasting marriage is no easy matter. It always was demanding and it always will be. After all, the idea that two individuals can interlock their lives in every area of their existence and yet stay together for what may easily be more than half a century, borders on the miraculous. Those couples who are setting out on such a journey need all the help and support they can get. In these talks there is much wisdom not just for the first months of married life but also for the long years that may, God willing, lie ahead.

These talks, given by different people at different times in different settings, have a common theme. Marriage is of God, it is a precious thing of blessing but it is also vulnerable. It is not to be taken for granted. Whether you are married or not, may what is written here help you understand marriage and value it more. And if you are a minister may these talks inspire you as you speak and preach at weddings.

J.John
Reverend Canon

1

PROCLAIMING MARRIAGE

Simon Allaby

One of the presents that my wife and I received when we got married was a toaster. The toaster came in a box with a set of instructions, but being of reasonable intelligence I never bothered to read them – it seemed fairly obvious where to put the bread and what to do with the dial on the front. All went well until we decided to toast some currant buns. I popped them in the toaster, pressed down the lever, and waited. After a few seconds there was a bang, and a small flame shot out from the top of the toaster. Upon investigation it turned out that a loose currant had fallen from the bun, become lodged between the element and the metal wall of the toaster and caused a short circuit. It was only at this point that I remembered the box in the loft with its list of instructions – and also, I hoped, a list of suppliers from whom I could order a new element. I duly found the instructions and as I started to read came across these words: 'When toasting currant buns, remove any loose currants from the bread before placing them in the toaster. Loose currants may fall into the appliance and damage the toaster.' My heart sank; if only I had read the instructions in the first place! But I hadn't thought that there was anything I needed to know.

It strikes me that we take the same approach to many things in life, and especially relationships – we just assume that it's all very obvious how to get along with someone else, and so we never stop to ask whether there are things that we do need to know – instructions, if you like, that would help protect and prosper the relationships we have with those we love. The Bible says that God is love and so, if there are things that we need to know, it is to him that we must look.

In his first letter to the church in Corinth, the apostle Paul writes about love in these well-known words:

> *Love is patient, love is kind. It does not envy, it does not boast, it is not proud. It does not dishonour others, it is not self-seeking, it is not easily angered, it keeps no record of wrongs. Love does not delight in evil but rejoices with the truth. It always protects, always trusts, always hopes, always perseveres. Love never fails.*
>
> *1 Corinthians 13:4–8*

It's a wonderful passage – but also potentially rather depressing! The standard of love that Paul describes is so high as to seem unattainable. If I'm honest I know that I have never loved anybody like this, and neither has anyone loved me in this way. It's that little word 'always' that is the problem; if Paul said that love 'sometimes' protects, trusts, hopes, etc., or even 'most of the time', I could somehow see myself attaining the standard that Paul sets. The clue to understanding Paul, however, is in realising that he is not describing human love at all, but rather the love of God – this is what God is like and this is how God loves us; and

Paul was quite sure of this (and so can we be) because of the life, death and resurrection of Jesus in which God's love for the world was made plain.

When we realise that love begins with God, and that his love for us is generous, sacrificial and limitless, two things become clear: first, that it is only God who can truly satisfy the longing of the human heart to be loved, accepted and cherished. No human heart has the capacity to satisfy this need, and if we look to our husband or wife to do so, then we ask of them something of which they are not capable. Secondly, if we receive this love from God and know that we are chosen, loved and accepted by him, then we are able to give it away and to follow his example of sacrificing ourselves on behalf of those we love.

It is sometimes said that marriage is a matter of 'give and take'. The Bible, however, paints a different picture – God loves us extravagantly but he does not take from us; rather, he invites us to respond and we do so by willingly giving our lives back to him. So, too, in marriage: if we receive God's love, we will give ourselves generously and sacrificially, honouring and cherishing our husband or wife – no need to take anything, and no need to worry that love will ever fail.

Simon Allaby is the founder and director of the 6:19 Trust. The Trust has the twin aims of seeing the Good News of Jesus proclaimed, and equipping and encouraging the church to evangelise. Simon was ordained in Durham in 1990 and has served as a full-time church leader in churches in Durham and Sussex. As part of his work with 6:19 Simon leads a church in Bolney, Sussex, where he lives with his wife and three children. For further information, see www.sixnineteen.co.uk.

2

IS LOVE ALL YOU NEED?
Doug Barnett

Reading: 1 Corinthians 13

A husband and wife were sitting reading – she deeply engrossed in her novel and he reading the newspaper. After a while the husband told his wife that he was reading an article about murder and hadn't realised there were so many different types, each with its own name. His wife, annoyed at being diverted from her book, said, 'Is that so?' and went on reading. Not deterred, her husband then proceeded to read out the various words – infanticide, homicide, regicide, matricide and genocide. Then he added, 'But it doesn't say what word they use when a wife murders her husband?' His wife looked up and said, 'It is called pesticide.'

Beneath the humour of the story lies an important truth – a wedding is a relatively short event but a marriage is a long-term, life-long love commitment.

The apostle Paul underscores the power and significance of love in relationships in 1 Corinthians 13 and ends up telling us, 'Now these three remain: faith, hope and love. But the greatest of these is love.'

Marriages may be made in heaven but they have to be worked out and lived out on earth. Today, it isn't your marriage that brings you joy and happiness but your love and commitment to each other. Let your love be more than an emotion that you feel for each other but a life commitment that you make to each other. Love makes allowances, believes the best and admits its mistakes. But having said all that, when it comes to marriage, 'Is love all you are going to need?' Yes, if you understand that love is not simply an emotion but also a decision that expresses itself in a number of ways.

1. Realism is essential

Marriage demands realistic expectations of each other because living together can be a tough experience; unloving and unlovable tendencies emerge in the finest people. A good marriage isn't when the perfect couple come together, it is when two imperfect people learn to accept and appreciate each other. It is about two weak people recognising that they need each other and together that they need God's help to make marriage work as it was intended to work.

2. Disagreements are normal

Marriage unites two people from different backgrounds and traditions and reveals that we do things differently, resolve issues differently and tackle relational problems differently. It is like two streams running down a mountainside. They run smoothly and quietly but when they converge there is noise, white water, bubbling, turbulence and a lot of spray. But further down the mountainside they run smoothly together as one. Adjusting to your new relationship will take time and disagreements will occur but that doesn't mean disaster. Differences of opinion are normal. They have to be worked out together. Remember, in the word 'wedding' 'we' comes before 'I'. Compromise will achieve far more than conflict, and slamming doors is less damaging than slamming each other. Marriages would be less volcanic if we learned the art of talking things through and sharing our feelings about things openly. Constructive communication can overcome destructive inner feelings.

If you can't seem to work through your disagreements then be wise and get help from trusted friends and your pastor. Above all, don't forget that the Lord who brought you together will help you to resolve the issues. Prayerfully seek his help and learn the truth that you will never be closer to each other than when you are individually close to God.

3. Encouragement should be mutual

Marriage is about affirming, supporting, encouraging and noticing things about each other. No one is ever deaf when praise is being offered and kind words spoken to them and about them. Look for things to commend in each other and refuse to focus on mistakes. It is said that Mrs Albert Einstein was once asked if she understood her husband's theory of relativity. 'No,' she said, 'but I know how he likes his tea.' Little things do mean a lot. Don't forget anniversaries, birthdays and the special events in family life. Express your appreciation to each other for the intention as well as the results.

Be considerate of each other. Don't be nicer to someone else's spouse than you are to your own – and speak well of each other in public.

4. Keep Jesus central

Proverbs 3:6 reminds us, 'In everything you do, put God first, and he will direct you and crown your efforts with success' (Living Bible).

Christianity is historical, verifiable, arguable, reasonable and involves an intelligent personal commitment to Jesus as Saviour and Lord. Jesus makes life make sense and he is the only third party in a marriage who can make it work better. Just as you have invited him into your life, now invite him into your marriage and you will discover that as life puts its pressures upon you – financially, with work issues, health concerns, family demands and personal anxieties – you will find Jesus is a constant friend and support, and as you trust him you will discover his loving commitment to you.

In the years ahead: may your love for each other grow and deepen; may your eyes always be open to see the best in each other; may your hands be outstretched to support each other; may your feet walk in step with each other; may you ever speak well of each other; and may Jesus always be central in your lives and marriage.

Doug Barnett is currently serving in an itinerant ministry of preaching, teaching and training in the UK, Middle East, India and Zambia. Married to Sue, they have two adult sons and two grandsons and two granddaughters. Doug has a special interest in the art of sermon illustration and is an avid soccer enthusiast and life-long supporter of Charlton Athletic soccer team.

3

SPECIAL CLOTHES FOR A SPECIAL DAY

Stuart Bell

One of the greatest moments in the life of a father is the wedding of a daughter. My daughter was soon to marry her fiancé and seemingly endless conversations were taking place with regard to preparations for the great day. Among the many issues discussed I want to concentrate on clothes. The Bell family and friends were all lined up to choose 'never to be worn again' clothes for the special day. I have to confess on occasions I was watching the till receipts increase as we all had to look our very best. Being challenged in terms of height I knew top hats were not necessary. No daughter wants to be given away by a small penguin. However, our daughter became the focus and the wedding dress was the priority. This took me back to the day I married my wife. In those days the choice was more limited but to this day that 'perfect for the day dress' still lies proudly in an old brown box in our wardrobe.

There is a beautiful passage of Scripture in Colossians 3:12–17. In *The Message* it reads, 'Dress in the wardrobe God picked out for you!' What a great thought! There are special clothes for special days. The apostle Paul then highlights five Christian virtues that ordinary people can clothe themselves with. He urges his readers to be clothed with compassion, kindness, humility, quiet strength and discipline. We all know that for a marriage to really work we need to look beyond the wedding day. However, the beauty of a wedding day can point us towards the potential beauty of lives brought together by God. Every marriage will face pressures and challenges. The virtues mentioned in this passage are so necessary for a healthy marriage. God has prepared a wardrobe for us. It seems that he wants to cover our weaknesses and help us to show compassion, kindness, humility, quiet strength and discipline. Paul then goes on to say, 'Regardless of what else you put on, wear love. It's your basic, all-purpose garment. Never be without it.' It's good to have special clothes for one special day, but God wants us to make the choice to love every day.

Perhaps 1 Corinthians 13 is the most popular passage read in Christian marriage services. I think this may be because new couples setting out on life's adventure together know how important love really is. 'Love is patient, love is kind . . . it always protects, always trusts, always hopes, always perseveres.'

Love on the outside

Our Colossians passage is so relevant to Christian marriage. Love needs to be 'put on'! Loving God and loving people are the two important things that Jesus asks of us. Love in marriage is what holds it together. How we speak to one another and honour one another will often determine our future. The passage goes on to say, 'Be even-tempered, content with second place, quick to forgive an offence. Forgive as quickly and completely as the Master forgave you.' Learning to forgive must be one of the main ingredients of a happy marriage.

Special clothes show us what is going on on the outside but what is happening internally can be very different.

Sadly, the beauty of a wedding day doesn't last. When I officiate in a wedding service I always say to a nervous bride before she goes down the aisle, enjoy every moment of this special day. Don't rush down the aisle, and make the most of every moment! The truth is that within a few days the groom standing at the front of the church will be in t-shirt and torn jeans, his hair will be dishevelled and his shining glow may have faded. A marriage needs more than outward clothes.

Peace on the inside

We often talk of 'inner beauty'. For those of us who were not blessed with great looks this brings encouragement. In Colossians 3 Paul moves his thinking from the outside to the inside. He says, 'Let the peace of Christ keep you in tune with each other, in step with each other' *(The Message)*. This is great advice for a newly married couple. This peace *(shalom)* is an inner beauty bringing health and well-being. In the pressures of life we need strength on the inside. This strength comes from God's word and places peace in our hearts. It is also very practical. Too many relationships are held back by a lack of peace. Often there are tensions in learning to live together. There are clashes of likes and dislikes which, left unchecked, can build resentment and hurt. The business of twenty-first-century life can create a pressure cooker of feelings waiting to explode. Marriage will never be argument-free but with good communication and God's help we can continually make progress. This passage continues, 'None of this going off and doing your own thing. And cultivate thankfulness.' I find myself in the blessed position of being married to the same woman for forty years. When I think of this fact I am very thankful. I am also thankful that my daughter and son-in-law remain happily married and that grandchildren increasingly demand my attention, but that's another story.

Stuart Bell is the senior leader of New Life Lincoln (www.newlifelincoln.org.uk). Stuart is also leader of the Ground Level Network, a network of over 100 churches. He works with a growing group of international leaders known as Partners for Influence. The group is missional and is working across different streams and denominations, bringing Kingdom perspectives and values. Their desire is to see strong, effective, healthy churches partnering together for greater influence. Stuart is a speaker and teacher and has written four books. Married to Irene, he has three children and three grandsons.

4

I'VE BEEN WAITING FOR YOU

Ray Bevan

The midday sun blazed on her tired body. She was tired with life, tired with people, tired with herself and tired of the snide remarks from the women in the village every time she went to draw water from the communal well. It's a long walk to draw the daily ration of water from Jacob's well, but the heat of the sun was more bearable than the fire in their tongues.

The women in the village had some basis for their attacks. She had experienced five divorces and the guy she was living with wasn't her husband. Perhaps the women in the village weren't so much judgemental as afraid. With her reputation all their husbands were at risk. She may have felt lonely but at least she had some peace. That was until she saw the Jewish rabbi sitting on the very well from which she was about to draw water. She was a Samaritan woman, at the bottom of the food chain. Her mind filled with all sorts of scenarios – more hassle, more judgement, more rejection. She was tired of it all. What a life-changing surprise to discover Mercy sitting at the well. One who knew the worst about her but was the last to judge her. What a heart-stopping moment when he began to talk to her, basically saying, 'Hi, I've been waiting for you.'

Nicodemus was a good man: intelligent, very religious and with integrity. He had a passion for God that could be seen. His fasting, prayers, knowledge and obedience to the law were immaculate. His meticulous desire to keep its 600+ disciplines was unequalled. He had a reputation that was faultless, a respect that was envious, but a heart that was empty. His religion wasn't working for him. His pursuit of righteousness always came up short. What was worse, he'd been listening to a carpenter from Nazareth claiming to have the words of eternal life. 'My yolk is easy and my burden is light.' Oh, how he longed to have a religion like that. His religion was weighing him down. One night, under the cloak of darkness, he went out quietly, as inconspicuous as possible. If anyone saw him talking to the preacher from Nazareth he would not only lose his friends but his influence as a teacher of the law. He arrived at the door, and knocked sheepishly. The door opened and he was face to face with the Miracle Worker, who lovingly looked at him with a smile that seemed to say, 'Hi, Nicodemus, I've been waiting for you.'

Peter's sobbing had stopped now; he was left with an aching in his gut that refused to go away. How could he have run away from his Saviour? To add to the disloyalty, there had been the denial! Not once, but three times and in the presence of ungodly people. His own words rang loud in his ears – 'I never knew him' – and the motive for those words stabbing deep at his guilty heart: to save his own skin. John's voice snapped him out of his guilt-ridden coma when he shouted, 'It is the Lord!' Not wanting to hear those words but at the same time longing to hear them, he dived fully clothed, headlong into the chilly morning waters and swam to the shore. Approaching the man cooking the fish he sat near the fire, head down, his eyes anywhere but into the eyes of the one he had betrayed. But nervously he looked up and their eyes met. His eyes were smiling and seemed to say, 'Hi, Peter, I've been waiting for you.'

As he hung on the cross he was just another thief paying for his crime. We don't know why he became a thief but whatever the reason it had now caught up with him and he knew, as they strapped him to the cross, that he had only a few hours to live. Turning to his right, he saw the Nazarene preacher. He'd heard him preach a few times but at that moment this dying thief realised this man not only had the answers to life but also death and beyond. With the revelation that this Nazarene preacher was from another world, he screamed, 'Remember me!' Jesus turned and said to him, 'Today you will be with me in Paradise.' It was no accident that this thief was crucified on that day, at that time and next to that man. It was as if Jesus was saying to him, 'Hi, I've been waiting for you.'

There was a groom and a bride. Independently they lived their lives not knowing of each other's existence. Both had travelled their own road of pain, joy, disappointment, tragedy and lost love. But one day their lives collided. They fell in love, decided to get married, made their plans and today they sit here filled with excitement, joy and perhaps a little anxiety – not knowing what the future may hold. But before they arrived at this marital altar, someone else was already here. The same one who sat at the well, waited behind a door, sat on a beach, died on a cross and who says to you the same words he said to the woman, the teacher, the failure and the thief: 'Hi, I've been waiting for you. As with the woman of Samaria, I'll always be waiting for you, even when others reject you. As with Nicodemus, I'll always be waiting for you when you're confused about life. As with Peter, I'll always be waiting for you, even when you fail me and, just as with the thief that day, I'll be waiting for you one day to take you home. Don't worry about tomorrow, I'll be waiting for you.'

Ray Bevan is a teacher, preacher, musician and singer. He has written a number of books which help anyone wanting to deepen their relationship with Jesus and fulfil their destiny. Together with his wife Laila, they pastor the Kings Church in Newport and have done so since 1989.

LOVE COMES FROM GOD

Gavin Collins

Reading: 1 John 4:7–12

Now when this couple asked me to give the address at their wedding today, at first I wasn't sure what I should talk about, and then I looked at the Bible reading that they'd chosen and I couldn't help noticing that it has the word 'love' thirteen times in just six short verses. So love it is – and what more appropriate subject could there be for a wedding day?

But what do we mean by 'love'? Are we right to say that love is flowers and chocolates and romantic moonlit walks? They are all good but actually, when we look back at our reading, we see that that sort of soppy sentimentality is not the kind of love that the Bible talks about. When we look at the Bible to get a Christian understanding of love, we see something very different. We see love demonstrated in tangible form, love that shows itself by way of commitment, sacrifice, self-giving and selflessness, a love that thinks in terms of 'you' – always putting the other person first – rather than of 'me' – my interests and my desires always needing to be satisfied; a love that is primarily about giving and only incidentally about receiving.

And the passage in 1 John illustrates this brilliantly. The first thing we see there is that: *'love comes from God'* (v.7) and what that means, throughout your marriage – in the bad times as well as the good – is that you can hold on to the certainty that because the love you have for each other is from God, then you can look to him to give you the strength to go on walking in that love. And God doesn't just give us the gift of love and leave us to get on and make the best use we can out of it. He steps down in human form and shows us what true love entails (vs.9–10).

So we see there that biblical love is unconditional. God loved us before we loved him – indeed, we are told elsewhere that God loved us even when we were actively opposed to him. And the love that showed itself in sending his Son Jesus to live and to die for us is sacrificial: it's costly; it's self-giving.

And as the passage continues, the challenge is set for us to live lives that display that same quality of love (vs. 11–12). And this is a challenge that's relevant to each one of us, whether we're married or single: *'Since God so loved us, we also ought to love one another.'*

And if that sounds like a tough challenge, then you're right: it is tough. In fact, it's impossible – humanly speaking, at least. Whatever the relationship, and however much we love another person, our pride and our selfishness will always get in the way and cause us to fall short of this standard. And if you try to build a marriage in your own strength, then at some point that will be true of you just as it is of every other human relationship.

And yet the great promise of the Bible is that God doesn't call us to live up to his standards in our strength alone. The very next verse says this: *'We know that we live in him and he in us: he has given us of his Spirit'* (v.13). We are given the Holy Spirit, the very power of God, to live in us, to help us and encourage us. And that means that unconditional, committed love is no longer some impossible ideal but rather, as we live in the very strength of God, it is a beacon, a signpost, that shows us the way to walk. And because our God is a forgiving God, when we do fall short and fail then the Spirit of God doesn't condemn or accuse us, but rather calls us to see where we've been at fault and gives us the humility to ask forgiveness and – if we're the one who's been wronged – gives us the grace to forgive.

So if we're living in the forgiveness that Jesus brings, the Holy Spirit in us both gives us the strength to aim for that standard of divine love and encourages us and helps bring restoration whenever we fail and fall short – which in our human fallibility we will inevitably do.

This passage goes on to acknowledge that there will be many problems in life – and also in marriage. There will be suffering, difficulty and pain. But if our life – if your marriage – is built on the kind of love that the Bible describes then it will be strong and endure, no matter what the difficulties. That knowledge can give us security and confidence at the very foundations of our lives, and of our relationships. As 1 John 4:18 says, *'There is no fear in love. But perfect love drives out fear.'* Again, the challenge is for each one of us – and in the vows you have made today you've made a very specific commitment to live this way, but all of us are called to live lives of this self-denying love. The challenge from today onwards – in the way we love each other – whether as husbands and wives, or in any other relationship – is to set an example for those around us of that Christ-like, self-giving, unconditional and very costly love.

So then, to sum up: as you make your marriage vows today, what's the biblical message? Love? Certainly. Schmaltzy romance? I hope not – or, at least, only as an aside, and when no one's looking! An easy life and a soft option? I think not, and the Bible never promises that. But God's continued blessing in your marriage, and God's strength in your life? That's guaranteed, and it's been demonstrated for all time on the cross of Christ, where God loved us so much that he gave his Son Jesus to die so that you, and I, and each one of us, might live.

Gavin Collins ministered for fourteen years in parish ministry in Cambridge and Chorleywood. He is currently the Archdeacon of the Meon in Portsmouth Diocese, where he is responsible for the care and support of fifty-five churches in south-east Hampshire. Gavin is married to Christina, a practice nurse, and they have three school-aged children. He is a life-long supporter of Brighton and Hove Albion FC. For more details, see www.portsmouth.anglican.org.

6

BUILDING A STRONG MARRIAGE

Mark Conner

Everybody loves a wedding and what a beautiful day it is for us to celebrate the marriage of our friends. Of course, a great wedding doesn't guarantee a great marriage. It takes time and effort to build on today's foundation and create a strong and healthy family (Proverbs 24:3–4). Thankfully, God has given us some helpful principles for that becoming a reality.

First of all, **have a strong commitment to each other.** In God's eyes, marriage is a covenant of love. It is a life-long agreement between a man and a woman. True love is much more than a feeling. It is a commitment based on one's vow, one's word and one's promise. Feelings come and go. Commitment stays the same.

Love each other as Jesus loves us (John 13:34). Jesus' loves never fails. He is committed to us no matter what. Character is the ability to carry out a good resolution long after the mood in which it was made is past. Long-lasting marriages are not necessarily problem-free, but the partners are committed to make it last. Make commitment, not feelings, the foundation of your marriage.

Secondly, **express appreciation to each other regularly.** Our words are very powerful (Proverbs 18:21). They can build someone up or tear a person down. Choose words that benefit each other (Ephesians 4:29). Express appreciation for each other regularly. Continually say positive things to one another. Be grateful. Notice and approve of what the other person does right. Don't be quick to criticise and slow to praise. We all thrive in an environment or atmosphere of encouragement and affirmation.

Thirdly, **have good communication.** Strong families spend a lot of time talking together. Good communication is what builds and maintains any relationship. When communication breaks down, so do families.

Good communication is one of the most important skills in life. We spend years learning how to read, write and speak but we often fail in effective *listening*. The apostle James once wrote, 'Be quick to listen, slow to speak and slow to become angry' (James 1:19). Instead, we are often quick to speak and slow to listen. God has given us two ears and one mouth so we should listen more than we speak. Be attentive to each other. Listen beneath the words to the meaning and the heart behind what has been said. Seek to understand. Be open with one another. Openness builds intimacy and closeness.

Fourthly, **spend a lot of time together.** Enjoy each other's company. You have spent a lot of time getting to know each other up to this point in your relationship. Keep building on that. Keep dating each other. Plan it —

enjoy life together. Continue to do things together. Making time for each other lets the other person know that they are important. While quality time is good, there is no substitute for quantity time.

Over-commitment and physical exhaustion are major marriage killers. The pace and pressures of life cause a lot of stress and pressure in relationships, especially when both partners are working, then coming home and relating out of left-over energy. Don't let that happen. Determine to make your relationship and your family a priority in your life.

Fifthly, **deal with problems in a constructive manner.** Deal with conflict in a positive way. Everyone has arguments, conflicts, crises and problems. They will happen. What we do about our problems is most important. The outcome will either hurt the relationship or help it. Families with the biggest problems don't necessarily break up. It's the way we respond to the problems that determines the future of the relationship. Problems confront every family and no one enjoys them, but strong families are able to respond to them in a constructive way. Conflicts cause strong families to pull together rather than be pulled apart, as they develop trust and a greater reliance on each other.

When conflict occurs, it is anger that gets us in trouble but it is pride that keeps us there. Never go to bed angry (Ephesians 4:26–27,31–32). You *will* get angry. But handle it right. Don't use anger as a weapon and don't hold on to it. Admit it when you are wrong. Take the initiative to resolve conflicts, even if you think you are right. Value being reconciled more than being right. Forgive one another.

Finally, **have a strong faith in God.** Spiritual vitality is the foundation of all good relationships. As we grow closer to God, he transforms us and we are empowered to love others more deeply. Make God the centre of your relationship. Two are better than one and a threefold cord is not quickly broken (Ecclesiastes 4:12). Lack of spiritual life is at the root of most relational problems. Pray together regularly (1 Thessalonians 5:17; 1 Peter 3:7). Serve God and go to church together.

Our prayer for you today is that this will be the beginning of a great future together. As you follow these principles, you can have a strong marriage. Enjoy the journey. God's grace will go with you. Good days are ahead.

Mark Conner is Senior Minister of CityLife Church, a diverse community of Christ-followers meeting in multiple locations in Melbourne, Australia. Mark is married to Nicole and they have three adult children. For more details, see www.citylifechurch. com; www.blog.markconner.com.au (Twitter: @MarkAConner).

7

THE THINGS I LOVE ABOUT . . .

Anthony Delaney

Reading: Colossians 3

What I have seen very clearly in the couples who seem to have what it takes to make a marriage that lasts is that it's most important that they have learned to be friends. Very good friends.

That's certainly true of these two. They've talked with me about how they know that God has brought them together. It's not an accident. I wonder what you think when they talk about God like that? If you know this couple then you'll know that this isn't about religion but relationship with God – it's a very personal thing for them. They believe what the Bible says about God, that he has a 'good and pleasing perfect plan' for our lives – and they want to live like they believe that's the case, putting him first today and in all their tomorrows together, because he's made himself so real to them in the past.

What kind of God do *you* think God is – if you ever think about God – and what do you think he thinks about you?

This couple can see how God has brought them together and brought them through to today, and they want *his* love – God's love – at the centre and surrounding *their* love.

So, right up front I'm going to tell you what the point of my message is. I want to invite everyone present to think again where you're at with God right now – and maybe that's enough of a challenge for some of you to just chew over. The big question is one you need to resolve: what if it's true? *What if they're right?*

It wasn't Jesus' great teaching or even his miracles that sent his earliest followers out on the street and enabled them to change the whole world in a couple of centuries. It wasn't that they were believers in some abstract philosophy. No – they were eyewitnesses to an event that changed everything. When Jesus died none of them really believed it could happen, but then . . . they saw him alive again. Met with him. Even ate with him. Nothing could stop these people! Everywhere they went they told everyone that God had done something unique in their lifetime: a man had been raised from the dead.

Now you may not believe that – and that's OK. But can I ask – have you thoroughly *investigated* it enough to be able to reject it? Because if it didn't happen it doesn't matter, but if it's *true* – nothing ever mattered more than that. It changes everything. It changes our priorities, our relationships, our past, present and future.

The apostle Paul writes about how we should live and love, married or single. In Colossians 3, he's talking about putting on a whole new set of clothes. You can understand that easily enough – lots of us have done that today. But these clothes just cover the outside; Paul's talking about how you can put on new attitudes, new actions, new thoughts – changing the *inside*, something a new hat or suit won't ever do. We buy something new and we think, 'That'll make me happy', but it never lasts. Before long it's 'that old thing!' It doesn't satisfy us and one day it ends up in the back of the wardrobe or at the charity shop. But Paul says (and I paraphrase), 'Because you know God *chose* you; because you know he *forgives* you; because you know God really *loves* you . . .' Then there's the invitation: 'Here are some new clothes – why not try them on?'

A tender heart – a heart that's responsive to others and full of compassion. *Kindness* – treating the other person kindly. Do you surprise your partner with kindness? When was the last time you did that? *Humility* – not being proud or pushy, not just thinking about yourself. *Patience* – or you could translate that as 'longsuffering'. So many marriages get shipwrecked because we're not patient with the other person. *Bearing with each other* – because nobody's perfect. Then it says *'Forgiving each other . . .'* There is no perfect marriage because there are no perfect people! At times we'll be let down and at times we'll let the other person down; we'll hurt them and be hurt. For better, for worse – that's what they said! If you're going to go the distance, you need to forgive the other person. How? Paul gives the answer: forgive each other just as Christ forgave you. And we are not meant to forgive grudgingly or half-heartedly. Paul knew Jesus Christ had given him a completely fresh start and a new life. And the people he was writing to knew that too. They knew that when Jesus was being crucified, nailed to a cross – in the most stunning act that silences critics thousands of years on – he didn't spit and curse like everyone else who died that terrible, torturous way but he cried out, 'Father – forgive them!' And if he forgave them – he'll forgive me. If he forgives me, he'll forgive you, too. If you ask him, he'll give you a fresh start in life. How do I know? Because it's what he came to do.

The final bit of clothing God offers? He says, 'Put on *love*, which ties it all together perfectly.'

Whatever you're wearing today at this wedding, it's as if God wants to put all those clothes on you. He's picked them out and they fit you perfectly. But you have to say, 'Yes, I'll put them on.' He doesn't force anyone. Are you wearing those clothes? When you are, you'll have an internal transformation of *peace* ruling in your heart. You'll have an attitude of gratitude. You'll be able to live wisely and joyfully. And unlike any other outfit, those clothes will never, ever wear out. And you can't buy them anywhere; Jesus already bought and paid for them for you 2,000 years ago.

Anthony Delaney leads Ivy Manchester, a church that meets in a cinema, a club, an inner-city estate, a warehouse and even a church building. Anthony features regularly on BBC Radio and at major conferences on issues of leadership, family life and personal development. He is the author of the men's book *Diamond Geezers* and also *The B.E.S.T. Marriage*. For more details, see www.ivymanchester.org.

8

A MARRIAGE THAT'S WORKING OUT!

Terry Eckersley

Reading: Romans 8:28

Welcome to the families, friends and colleagues of the bride and groom. We are all here to celebrate and encourage the couple's obvious love for one another and their decision for holy matrimony.

A minister was preparing a couple for their wedding day. The very nervous and excited bride repeatedly kept on getting the order of service mixed up. The minister made it simple for her:

First, you walk down the aisle.
Second, you stop at the altar.
Third, we all sing a hymn together.

This really helped ease the bride. So, on the day in question, she walked down the aisle repeating these three words: Aisle, Altar, Hymn; Aisle, alter him; I'll alter him!

My first bit of friendly advice is that marriage is not about altering or changing the other person, but – biblically – we do change to accommodate our partner, preferring one another in love. When God in his infinite wisdom saw it was not good for man to be alone, he chose to give him a help mate, which translates 'perfect fit'! Not perfect, but a perfectly fit wife! While on our own we don't have it all together, in marriage we have everything.

> *And we know that in all things God works for the good of those who love him, who have been called according to his purpose. For those God foreknew he also predestined to be conformed to the image of his Son, that he might be the firstborn among many brothers and sisters. And those he predestined, he also called; those he called, he also justified; those he justified, he also glorified. What, then, shall we say in response to these things? If God is for us, who can be against us? He who did not spare his own Son, but gave him up for us all – how will he not also, along with him, graciously give us all things?*
> *(Romans 8:28–32)*

I believe these verses are so appropriate for today, for life and for marriage; for me this is one of the pinnacles of the apostle Paul's teaching. In today's world of uncertainty, with nations in conflict and relationships and marriages under pressure, we can learn so much from this for the rest of our – and especially the bride and groom's – special day and lives.

1. Have a confident and good marriage (Romans 8:28)

'And we know that in all things God works for the good of those who love him.' How cool is that. We can have a confidence knowing that in *all* things, as long as we love God, we have the promise and assurance that everything is going according to schedule, to plan, and God himself makes it clear that we can *know* this, can be assured, unmoved, and have a confident marriage.

2. Have a purposeful marriage (Romans 8:28)

'Called according to his purpose.' God promises you a marriage full of purpose, meaning and direction, with a reason for living and giving. A marriage that isn't just about you, but about the plans and purposes God has for you. Remember this today and tomorrow, during the ups and the challenges. God Almighty has a great purpose for your lives, and while one will put one thousand to flight, two will put ten thousand to flight! Do the maths – together you will be purposefully much more powerful.

3. A fully inclusive marriage (Romans 8:29)

'For those God foreknew he also predestined to be conformed to the image of his Son.' You have a fully inclusive marriage deal; God has predestined it! Not only is it to be confident and good, but it has been tailor made, a designer marriage, made by the greatest craftsman ever! That's why they call him God. Your destiny is a confident, good and predestined marriage. Remember this today, tomorrow and for the rest of your lives. God has got it *all* under control, as we learn to love and trust and depend on him and one another.

4. A justified marriage (Romans 8:30)

'Those he called, he also justified.' Of course, as we know and can see, the main reason, the justification for your marriage today is love. That wonderful virtue, gift, feeling, noun: love is a doing word. God is love: 'For God so loved the world that he gave his one and only Son, that whoever believes in him will not perish [wither, rot] but have eternal life' (John 3:16). God has justified you and we who believe. Justification means just as if we never sinned – holy, acquitted in heaven's courts, clean, spotless. We are likened to the bride and her dress: clean, spotless, all because of the redemptive work that Jesus did on the cross when he who was no sin, became sin, that we might be the righteousness, the justified of God. Have a justified life and marriage.

Marriage prayer

So let's all stand as we pray for this wonderful couple that they might have a confident, loving, purposeful marriage.

Understanding, Lord Jesus, that you have joined them together, to a fully inclusive marriage plan, predestined before the foundation of the world. A marriage that has been called and justified by you. We bless them and commit them and their future to you, knowing it is all working out together for your good and your glory according to your will and word. We also accept your justification, your sacrifice for us, that we now can be a loving Christian family and friends. Today, and always. Let your name be glorified in our lives and in this marriage, in the mighty and all-powerful name of Jesus. Amen.

Terry Eckersley is a creative communicator with an appeal that transcends all cultures, people groups and denominations. To date, he has completed many speaking, media, radio and TV engagements at churches, conferences and prisons in several countries. Terry has published books, songs and music.

9

LOVE ME WITH ALL YOUR HEART

David Hall

Our warmest congratulations on this very special day. We wish you all the best for the future. And with the future in mind, we are looking together at a wonderful reading from the Bible, from the Song of Solomon 8:6–7. This is a very appropriate poem on a happy occasion like this. It's a speech by a young bride to her husband-to-be, King Solomon – God's anointed king over Israel, but a frail human being like you and me. Not unusually he needs to be told what to do by his wife. I think you'll all agree that's a very good start to marriage!

The central message of this passage is 'Love me with all your heart' – a bride is saying it to her groom and God is also saying it to his people. But as the appeal is made, we realise how much the person making the appeal deeply loves the one they are speaking to. We realise how much this bride must have loved Solomon and how much God loves us; and we learn four things about God's love.

1. Private and public

God's love is private and public: 'Place me like a seal over your heart, like a seal on your arm . . .' (v.6). The heart is private and the arm is public. There is a public and private dimension to married love: there are the publicly declared vows, but there will also be whispered thoughts and expressions, for each other only.

It is often moving to see a newly married couple kneeling in prayer after their vows, with the symbolic suggestion that as well as being together as a couple, they can draw near to God in a quiet, personal way.

Do we yearn for a personal relationship with the loving, living God? God appeals to us also to show such public and private love for him. He, in the most public way imaginable, created the universe, even died on the cross, to show his love for us. There are also public occasions, like today, when we sing hymns of praise publicly to him or join together in the Lord's Prayer. But there needs to be a personal relationship, a quiet awareness that he is a personal God who has drawn near to us and revealed himself to us.

2. All-consuming

God's love is all-consuming: 'For love is as strong as death, its jealousy unyielding as the grave. It burns like blazing fire, like a mighty flame . . .' (v.6). Can anyone ever love someone that much? One of the remarkable things about marriage is that two people, who once were strangers, can now love each other with such intensity. Does God love us with this kind of intensity? Yes, the Bible says, his love for us is as strong as death.

In John's Gospel we read, 'God so loved the world that he gave his one and only Son, that whoever believes in him shall not perish but have eternal life' (John 3:16). In short, God gave his Son to die so that, coming to him in sorrow for our sins and in obedient friendship, we might live.

The couple today walked through the graveyard as they entered the church to be married. And the old life they lived before is now dead and buried; they have a new life together as husband and wife. And so it is with God's love for us. He has loved us and died so that we can live. We can bury the past, make a fresh start and enjoy a new life with him, eternal life.

3. Eternal

God's love is eternal: 'Many waters cannot quench love; rivers cannot sweep it away' (v.7). In other words, God's love is not fickle and short-term.

It's really inspiring to meet couples who are celebrating fifty years or more of married life. I read of one couple celebrating their Golden Wedding Anniversary who were asked what their secret was. The husband said, 'A row every day; it made things more interesting!'

The important thing about love is to keep going! Because God has kept loving us. In Jeremiah 31:3, God is quoted as saying to his people: 'I have loved you with an everlasting love; I have drawn you with unfailing kindness.' We can't shock God: he already knows the worst about us and has chosen to love us faithfully, but it is a love we have often ignored, with painful consequences.

4. Cannot be bought

God's love cannot be bought: 'If one were to give all the wealth of one's house for love, it would be utterly scorned' (v.7).

There are many bills associated with a wedding, but the one thing you can't buy is love. It is freely given and it is beyond price. You and I cannot earn God's favour. We cannot buy his love for us with good deeds. In our natural state we are helpless before a holy God. Yet uniquely Jesus Christ was able to pay the price. He died that we might live. We receive loving forgiveness and new life as a free gift through trusting in him and putting him first in our marriage and in our lives.

In conclusion, as we celebrate today with this appeal from a bride to her husband, let me challenge us all with this thought: God has loved us with all his heart. And the appeal of this bride echoes his appeal to us: 'Love me with all your heart.'

There is a private and public dimension to God's love for us and our response to him. His love is also all-consuming, eternal and cannot be bought. God's love is a gift for every person at this wedding, waiting to be received. Wouldn't it be great not just to come to a wedding and rejoice with the bride and groom but to come to a wedding and receive from God a gift, the gift of eternal life?

David Hall is Vicar of Christchurch Chorleywood. He has both British and Swiss nationality and was brought up in Norfolk. His first degree was in Business Studies. During his university vacations, he worked for the Royal Household at Buckingham Palace and Balmoral Castle and was attacked by the corgis during a blizzard in the grounds of Sandringham House before being rescued by the Queen. He is married with four children.

10

LOVE THAT LASTS

Greg Haslam

Reading: Ephesians 5:22–33

Today's the day! Some days you wait a short time for, others rather longer. The longer the wait, the greater the prize! These two would agree with that. We're all here because we love them and share their joy in anticipating a long, fruitful marriage.

We have here a man of integrity, fun and courage. A God-lover, a man's man, and one who knows a good woman when he finds one! And we have a woman who is intelligent, beautiful, charming and talented. They're both people-persons – warm, hospitable, creative, truly faithful friends with a big heart for God and people. God has brought them together.

Loneliness is difficult to bear. In Genesis 2, in Eden, God saw Adam's loneliness and decided to address it. Adam freely enjoyed all the wonders of paradise. After the gardening, then naming all the animals . . . he became lonely and dissatisfied! He wanted company. Real company – not giraffes, tigers or monkeys. A creature he could talk to and impress!

God said, 'I see you're lonely. I'll make a perfect woman for you.' 'What's a woman?' Adam asked. God said,

'A woman will love and adore you. She'll cook perfect meals and always look gorgeous. She'll laugh at your jokes and never complain!' Adam said, 'That's wonderful! But she sounds expensive. What will she cost?' God replied, 'A woman like that could cost you an arm and a leg!' God always tells the truth! Adam considered this carefully for a moment, then asked his Maker, 'What could I get for just one spare rib?'

This couple were once alone. Not completely alone; they both have many friends. But something important was missing from their lives: one another. Those of us who know them can see they're so right for each other, with lots in common: great personalities, love for God, solid faith, kind, generous and with love for each other. It's great to know we're loved. Ephesians deals with this in these powerful paragraphs. The church, the whole of God's people, is like a bride. The bridegroom is Jesus. He's 'married' to us, and he loves messed-up sinners more than anybody else does. We love him in return! This models a husband's love for his wife, and her reciprocal love for him.

Paul addresses husbands first. The husband's charge is probably the hardest to maintain – because men are men! We're so selfish, insensitive – even stupid! We have distorted views of manhood, from the playboy James Bond to the action hero Jason Bourne. Instead of all that nonsense, husbands are told to, 'Love your wives as Christ loved the church and gave himself up for her.' Jesus is your role model. That's why we say vows. You're promising God you'll do this.

In early English marriages, the wife promised her husband that she would be, 'Bonny and buxom, in bed and at board' as authorized by the Bishop of Salisbury in 1095! Bonny is from the French for good, and buxom is from the German for 'pliant' or 'sweetly respectful'. Such a bride is very special and in order to help a wife be so she should be loved a lot. What does this love look like?

1. It's freely chosen (v.23). Out of a universe of creatures, Jesus chose the church! We were personally chosen by the Lord to be his. No one forced him. God looked down the future centuries, and then chose us to be loved and saved. Love is first of all a choice and decision before it's a 'falling in love'. In fact, we can't sustain romantic love without choosing and maintaining that decision to love, no matter what!

2. It's happy, contented (v.31). The word 'marriage' signifies 'merry age'. It's designed by God to make you both happy! It implies we like each other, and want rich companionship. 'Things' can't make us happy. House, hi-fi, 50" TV, car and lots of cash in the bank can't do it. Only God, that special person, and friends can make us truly happy! That's God's idea!

3. It's sacrificial, selfless (v.25b). Christ knew the cost of obtaining his bride. He gave himself up for her in a violent death, spilling his life through wounds in his hands, feet, head and body. He lost pints of blood, so we could escape death. A husband sacrifices for his wife. We'd willingly die for our wives but the biggest sacrifice is to live for them! Give her your support, wisdom, love and time.

4. It's also regularly spoken (v.26). Marriages decay when couples cease to communicate. Christ gave a long 'love letter' in the Bible. We read all the lines, and then read between the lines to hear his voice. In addition, we hear his voice through preachers, prophetic people and his 'inner' voice in our hearts. Talk to each other. You'll get to like it!

5. It's warm, healing (v.26). A 'saving' love rescues us from bad things.

6. It's affectionate, demonstrative (v.27). Men are often lame at this, except when we're looking after ourselves! Nothing is too difficult, too expensive, too time-consuming, too far away, too demanding, when it concerns men! We pamper, bathe, reward, and nurse ourselves better when we're ill – 'man-flu' can kill us! Men look in a mirror and say, 'Looking good!' They eat often, sleep deeply, buy cool outfits, drive great cars; even a 'bit of a paunch' or 'bald patch' won't phase them too much. Treasure your wife. Many men struggle even to be kind. Hugs. Kisses. Regular sexual relations. Gifts of cards, cinema tickets, cappuccinos, treats. My advice is to try praising your wife even if it does frighten her a bit at first! Look after her spiritual welfare too.

A good marriage means that you fall in love again and again during your lifetime – always with the same person! Christ is not a fickle lover, nor should we be. Couples in love enter a long-term investment with great rewards. This is what we mean by 'love that lasts'.

Greg Haslam is Minister of Westminster Chapel in London. He travels widely as a Bible teacher and conference speaker. He has a heart to bring Word and Spirit together through a biblical theology. Greg is married to Ruth and they have three grown-up sons and three grandchildren. He is the author of seven books.

11

WEDDING AT CANA

Graham James

It's a delight to be with you all today. There is nothing better than a wedding to cheer people up. It's a statement of hope in the future. It tells us that human beings are made for love. Love and not fear lies at the heart of this world.

We have been reminded that Jesus was a guest at a wedding in Cana of Galilee. That was the setting for his first miracle. It's about twenty years since I visited Cana. Even now it is a rather modest village but they do sell rather grim *vin ordinaire* at inflated prices in honour of Jesus' first miracle. Take advice from this bishop: don't buy it.

As it was, this first miracle of Jesus was born out of necessity. The drink ran out at the reception. Hundreds of gallons of water were turned into wine. I am sure the bride's parents have made sure the arrangements at today's reception are rather better ordered – best not to rely on such a miracle.

There have always been a few sour-faced people who really disapprove of this first miracle of Jesus. It seems a bit trivial, a bit self-indulgent. Why would the Saviour of the world concern himself with the supply of wine? Why didn't Jesus begin his work by healing the sick or declaring a mission for world peace? This miracle makes the straight-laced uneasy and it confounds atheists with its sheer joy and exuberance.

Jesus was spreading delight. That's what we are here to do today. We celebrate the delight that this couple are being joined together so that they become, as the Scriptures put it, *'one flesh'.* That's a miracle even more significant than water turning into wine. Today we celebrate the miracle that love is at the heart of our world. It isn't a theory. It isn't something that would be nice if only it were real. Love is at the heart of the world because it is expressed by human beings belonging to each other in the most intense, mysterious and joyful way.

So today we come to take delight in two people's love for each other. You cannot persuade yourself to love someone. These two have found they cannot live without one another. They are going to declare in public their love for each other. That gift of love is a gift from God. St John says, *'Whoever lives in love lives in God, and God in them'* (1 John 4:16).

Marriage matches love with promises. That's the tough bit. The bride and groom will promise today to be faithful, constant and reliable with each other. And because they are going to be like that with each other the hope is they will be even more faithful, constant and reliable with the rest of us. That's why we are here. Marriage doesn't happen in private. It is incredibly public. You have all been invited but this is simply a public act of worship in this church. Anyone can come. And that's important. We change all our relationships when we get married, our relationships with each other, with the families of which we are a part, with our friends and with the rest of society.

Two families are coming together today. The bride and groom will in future have those wonderful things called in-laws: mothers-in-law, fathers-in-law, brothers-in-law, sisters-in-law. I think it's a pity we give law the credit. We ought to give love the credit but I suppose if we had a sister-in-love or a father-in-love people might get the wrong idea. Even so, it's not just two people who are extending their relationships today. When we marry someone we take on a whole network of other human relationships that come with them. That's testing. It challenges our selfishness. A new family is given to us.

But there is something more – restrictions on freedom. This couple are going to tell us in a minute or two that because of their love for each other they no longer simply want to do whatever they wish. They will pledge that they will exclude other sexual relationships. In marriage you cannot simply do what you want. You make a pledge to think and care for each other. At its best, marriage should make us more thoughtful people.

There is something else they are doing today. They are taking on each other's histories. They are young compared with this white-haired bishop but they are old enough, both of them, to have a past. You cannot blot out your past when you get married. You are who you are because of what has happened in your life. They probably think they know one another very well already. I have now been married for over thirty-four years – and to the same woman.

It helps in my profession. Since she is here in the congregation I had better be careful what I say but I know that even now we have plenty more to learn from each other. Human beings develop and change. There is always more to discover. There is always more to forgive. As today's bride and groom will find, the best marriages are nurseries of love and cradles of forgiveness. None of us will be married happily for very long unless we master the art of saying sorry.

When Jesus attended that wedding at Cana in Galilee he preached no sermon. He gave no speech. He didn't tell the couple how to get the best out of their relationship. He didn't do any of these things. He simply concerned himself with the supply of wine. It seemed a shame to him if anything was lacking which could spread delight around.

No wonder the image of God's kingdom of love and peace in the Gospels is often one of a marriage banquet, a feast, a great celebration of eternal life and love. We pray today that the best wine of God's blessing may be this couple's joy for the rest of their lives.

Graham James is the Bishop of Norwich. He was ordained in 1975, worked in Welwyn Garden City as a team vicar and then moved to Church House, Westminster where he had responsibility for overseeing the selection procedures for candidates for ordination in the Church of England. In 1987 he was appointed as Chaplain to the Archbishop of Canterbury (Robert Runcie) and continued to work as Archbishop's Chaplain with George Carey during his first two years in office. Graham is married to Julie, a staff nurse, and they have two adult children.

12

WEDDING CLOTHES

J.John

Reading: Colossians 3

It is a privilege to speak to you as a married couple and to give you some personal advice publicly!

When a little girl came out of Sunday school, her mum asked her what they had been learning. 'Well,' she said, 'the teacher told us about how God made the first man and the first woman. He made the man first, but he was very lonely with nobody to talk to, so God put him to sleep, and while he was asleep, God took out his brains and made a woman out of them.'

Let me give you the right version: 'Eve was not made out of Adam's head to rule over him, nor out of his feet to be trampled upon by him, but out of his side to be equal with him, under his arm to be protected, and near his heart to be loved.'

Well. Here you are, all dressed in your wedding finery. Marriages are made in heaven, but we are responsible for the maintenance work. How do we dress for success in a marriage? What are you going to wear to ensure that yours will be enduring and satisfying? In the reading St Paul gives advice for a marriage wardrobe.

1. Clothe yourselves with compassion. Compassion means 'a heart of empathy'. A feeling and an action in response to someone's need. Make sure you don't see through one another, but see one another through. Maturity grows when you can sense your concern for each other outweighing your concern for yourselves.

2. Clothe yourselves with kindness. Kindness is the oil that takes the friction out of life. As the sun makes ice melt, kindness causes misunderstanding and hostility to melt. Always think how you can lighten the burden for each other. You cannot do a kindness too soon, because you never know how soon it will be too late. Kind hearts are the garden. Kind thoughts are the roots. Kind words are the blossom. Kind deeds are the fruits.

3. Clothe yourselves with humility. If ever there is an arena where pride and the need to be right occur, it's in a marriage. There is a story about two mountain goats that met each other on a narrow ledge, just wide enough for one of them to pass. On one side there was a sheer cliff and on the other side a steep wall. The two of them were facing each other and it was impossible to turn or to back up. How did they solve their dilemma? One of them lay down and let the other walk over them and both were safe. A wise lesson from two goats!

A good motto:

> *To keep your marriage brimming,*
> *With love in the wedding cup,*
> *Whenever you're wrong, admit it;*
> *Whenever you're right, shut up.*

Humility is not thinking less of yourself, but thinking of yourself less.

4. Clothe yourselves with gentleness. Gentleness is the garment of sensitivity to others' thoughts and feelings. To be gentle means to be understanding. Gentle people are not demanding. When you express gentleness, the other person can take off any self-defensive armour or fearfulness, and can put on trust.

5. Clothe yourselves with patience. A man read to his wife that researchers had found that women use twice as many words per day as men. The wife replied that was because they had to repeat everything twice to men. To which the husband responded, 'I'm sorry, what was that?'

Patience and understanding fit together. 'Understand' is an interesting word. To 'stand under': this implies that you need to experience what your spouse feels – standing under their circumstances and in their situation – then you will be more patient with each other.

6. Clothe yourselves with forgiveness. You can bury a marriage with a lot of little digs. Forgiveness means to erase, to release resentment, to wipe the slate clean. And remember, once you have forgiven each other, don't re-heat the error for breakfast. The four hardest statements to make in marriage are: 'I was wrong'; 'I am sorry'; 'I don't know'; and 'I need help'. I urge you to use those four statements with each other when necessary, as they will build integrity and honesty in your marriage.

If compassion is marriage's inner garment – and if kindness, humility, gentleness, patience and forgiveness are its outer garments – then love is the overcoat.

'On top of all these things,' St Paul says,

7. 'Put on love.' Love keeps a marriage warm. Happy marriages begin when we marry the ones we love, and they blossom when we love the ones we marry. Love as an emotion can wear thin and threadbare when feelings ebb. Love, as the overcoat that keeps a marriage warm, is made up of two things, both of which must be there for marriage to endure: commitment and caring.

'I will be there for you.' That's the commitment you make with your vows. But what good is commitment without caring? Caring says, 'I commit myself to you. I will be there for you.'

The Christian custom of placing a wedding ring on the third finger began with the early Greeks. They believed that the 'vein of love' ran from the third finger directly to the heart. When you put those rings on each other's fingers part of you is symbolically saying that you want to be tied right into their heart. You want to be committed to each other.

From the story of the wedding in Cana we learn three things: bring our needs to Jesus; offer him what we have; and do whatever Jesus says.

So to conclude, a recipe for marriage:

To a bowlful of compassion add:
a cup of kindness,
a generous spoonful of humility,
a dose of gentleness,
several cups of patience
and a large measure of forgiveness.
To bind all this together, keep on adding love.

Raise your expectations
and your expectations will raise you.
Anticipate success
and success will anticipate you.

J.John lives in Chorleywood, Hertfordshire in England. He is married to Killy and they have three sons, Michael, Simeon and Benjamin. J.John is a speaker with an appeal that transcends gender, age, race, culture and occupation. To date, he has completed thousands of speaking engagements in sixty-nine countries on six continents. J.John has also authored several titles. For more details, see www.philotrust.com (www.twitter.com/Canonjjohn).

13

MARRIAGE – I DO!

Simon McIntyre

I love marriage. We all love marriage. That is why we are all here today. Marriage pivots much of our lives. We are either looking forward to it, have just started one, are in the middle of one, have sadly lost one, or wish we could get out of one. You name it, someone is facing it.

And the statistics for marriage longevity are hardly encouraging. Yet somehow we still love a good wedding. A good marriage is wonderful. We all want one. And we all start with that in mind.

I believe in marriage – I do! Empathically and joyfully. I believe in the ceremony of marriage, where we say our vows to each other before God, and before others. Jesus did too. His first recorded miracle was at a wedding and had no other purpose than to make sure a good marriage celebration continued to be one. How good was that?

Marriage is a community event and that is part of its secret; a secret soon forgotten in a world where the individual reigns supreme – and woe to anyone who suggests otherwise. The ancient 'landmark' of the marriage ceremony is very important. Why?

We aren't capable of sustaining vows and promises unless we do them in an environment of accountability.

Our friends and family are vital witnesses to both our promises and our potential weaknesses. That's what they are here for – to care, and to hold us to our word. This is not a veiled threat but a great encouragement.

Let's be sure to pray for this couple as they embark on this life-changing, life-defining journey, 'Lord, bless and keep them.'

And what defines a marriage? We need go no further than the words of Scripture, where it is said in Genesis 2:24, 'This explains why a man leaves his father and mother and is joined to his wife, and the two are united into one' (NLT). This verse essentially defines a marriage with three elements that we reject or minimise to our own loss.

Firstly, a man and woman are to *leave* their parents and make a new social unit. Their parents are not to interfere and every time they do a marriage is put under immense strain, to the point of breaking, if this is not recognised and dealt with. A man who never 'leaves' his family to create a new one creates terrible uncertainty and anxiety in his new wife. And you have to ask what kind of man he is? I knew of a young man who was hounded by and counselled by his mother. He also sought her opinion and assurances. He got them but not surprisingly he lost his wife. She hadn't agreed to be married to his mother as well. Rightly so.

Secondly, in this verse from Genesis it is stated they are *to be joined*. A marriage needs a joining purpose and vision that is more compelling than just being a couple. Being a couple is terrific but it isn't enough. Having 'joined' you need to have an outward-looking view. For me it has always been God's house – his church. My marriage is about more than our preferences and goals, and always has been – thankfully for my wife. Doing compelling things together helps you stay together, and enjoy each other.

Thirdly and finally, a marriage needs, unequivocally, a healthy sex life. It is no marriage without this. Sexual connection and fun – did I say fun? – is breath to your lungs, except when it exhausts you. Interestingly Adam and Eve had no clothes, nor any embarrassment when together. A man and woman should be able to be naked without shame – on the contrary!

A marriage in which someone deliberately withholds or ignores any of these three elements is bound for struggle alley or possibly even the divorce courts. There may be seasons when one or more of the three elements are unable to be fulfilled, such as when a man or woman may be overseas on military duty, or when a sickness interposes itself upon a family. But otherwise it is no real marriage without these three parts in working order.

Marriage – I do! Do you?

Simon McIntyre, along with his wife Valerie, is the pastor of C3 London, overseer of C3 Churches in Europe/UK and a director of C3 Global (see www.c3london.com). His church background is rich and varied and he identifies his gift as 'doing what needs to be done'. Simon is a great fan of and believer in the church. When time allows he flies an aerobatic plane, writes books and sits on a beach – not all at the same time.

14

MARRIAGE AFTER DIVORCE

Allan Meyer

We welcome you all and thank you for being here to share in new beginnings. I have been given the privilege of choosing the Bible reading for the wedding address so I want to draw your attention to the book of Genesis, where the origin of marriage is described: 'So God created mankind in his own image, in the image of God he created them; male and female he created them' (Genesis 1:27).

God accepts responsibility for the creation of gender. Our sexuality is not the end product of a mindless mechanistic universe – it was formed deliberately by the mind of God and with this purpose in mind: 'That is why a man leaves his father and mother and is united to his wife, and they become one flesh' (Genesis 2:24).

Marriage is central to the very nature of God and to the nature of life itself. Many see marriage as a human institution – the product of social evolution, invented by people to normalise family life and relationships. Not so. In fact, there has never been a recorded civilisation in human history in which marriage was unknown as a foundational relationship in some form. Marriage is not the end product of social evolution; it is divine in origin and purpose. It is a human institution in that human beings are the ones who marry but its origin is to be found in the heart of God and it is woven into the hearts of people made in his image.

I'm impressed by the reflections of Jesus on this very thought. Marriage is problematic. We all want to be loved. We all need to be loved and when we are loved it makes a world of difference. It is this inner cry for love and intimacy that drives us to marriage, yet it is a relationship with many demands and challenges – so much so that one of the questions of Jesus' day was, 'How hard should it be to get a divorce?' Jesus responded by reminding his listeners of the words of Genesis and then added his own postscript: 'What God has joined together, let no one separate' (Mark 10:9). Jesus saw marriage as a God-kind of joining. It is the invention of God; it flows from the purposes of God and, as such, all should hold it in profound reverence.

The longing to be loved, to be known and treasured, to be intimately joined to another is a God-kind of longing and marriage is the God-kind of response that brings you two here today. I want to commend both of you today for your courage. You have both known the pain of a marriage to which you were deeply committed coming to an end.

I know there will be those who see you here today, stepping again into this God-kind of joining, who will ask themselves, 'Why do this again?' I know why you are coming to this altar again: the hope of love is compelling, and you have the courage to believe it can be found through Christ in this life and the next. I, for one, join you in that confidence.

I know there will be those who see you here today wondering whether it should even be happening. 'Marriage is a God-kind of joining and the Bible tells us that God hates divorce. Should this be happening in church?' There should be no safer place to rebuild your future than in church. There is no one who understands your journey better than God himself. Marriage proceeds from God's heart – and God always saw his relationship with his people as a marriage. The church is called the bride of Christ and his return is called a wedding feast. Jeremiah wistfully speaks for God, the broken-hearted groom, as he remembers the drawing of Israel to himself out of Egypt. Hear the heart of a wounded husband – like a grieving husband looking back over the wedding photos taken years before: 'I remember the devotion of your youth, how as a bride you loved me and followed me through the wilderness' (Jeremiah 2:2).

God saw his devotion to Israel as a marriage. Hear his poignant question, reflecting years of painful struggle: 'What fault did your ancestors find in me, that they strayed so far from me?' (Jeremiah 2:5). Hear his anguished resolution as the marriage comes to a heart-breaking end: 'I gave faithless Israel her certificate of divorce and sent her away because of all her adulteries' (Jeremiah 3:8).

God hates divorce at least in part because he has been through one. God himself is a divorcee, testifying to the fact that no matter how hard one partner to a marriage might try, one alone cannot make it permanent. Even God was unable to make that marriage last. He knows the hurt, the disappointment and the loss. The house of God is the safest place in the world to rebuild your future – your heavenly Father has walked this pathway too.

Why hope for this marriage? Because I know the spirit in which you come now to be joined. I know something of your journey and how earnestly you sought to honour your marriage vows. I have watched you bring your loss to the throne of God in humility and faith. I have watched you process the challenge of forgiveness by embracing Christ at the foot of the cross. I have watched as you have brought the possibility of this new beginning to God in humility and faith. I have watched courage and confidence reborn as your journey together was laid in the hands of Jesus. You have the testimony of your own heart, you have the testimony born of prayer, you have the testimony of counsellors who have journeyed with you and confirm your readiness for new beginnings.

Today, in the presence of God and of this company, we join with you in hope of a life that will honour Christ and be a blessing to all. We commit you to each other and the grace of God with this promise: 'Behold, I make all things new.'

Allan Meyer pastored Careforce Church for twenty-six years. While leading Careforce he and his wife Helen founded the ministry of Careforce Lifekeys, focusing on restoring broken lives. The Lifekeys ministry has spread to churches all over Australia and New Zealand with churches all over the world using the programs for discipleship, church health and evangelism. Allan's doctoral project was the creation of another Lifekeys program called Valiant Man, a program to restore and fortify the moral and spiritual integrity of men. Allan and Helen now devote their energy to coaching and equipping churches to function effectively as restoring communities. For more details, see www.careforcelifekeys.org.

15

REMEMBER TODAY

Nigel Mumford

Readings: Ruth 1:16–17; John 15:9–12

I have thoroughly enjoyed getting to know you both and we rejoice with you on this memorable day.

For the groom, it is vitally important that you remember today's date for the rest of your life – never, ever forget that, my friend! Groomsmen, part of your job for the rest of your life is to remind this man at least a week before.

I always ask those coming for marriage counselling three questions: do you like each other; do you love each other; and are you friends? For it is friendship that endures in marriage. Also, I always ask them where they 'squeeze the toothpaste tube'. I have found over the years that this can be a cause of friction within a marriage. For the most part, men squeeze it from the bottom and women squeeze it near the middle . . . or, even worse, the top. This can be an instant cause for a very petty argument.

In their pre-marital counselling I found out that this bride sure enough squeezes the tube from the middle and the groom squeezes it from the end. Therefore, my counsel is that they each have their own tube of toothpaste – for the rest of their lives. This is my marital 'healing prescription' to all of you who have 'toothpaste tube issues'. Get your own tube! Today at the reception, if you introduce yourself to someone, do give your name and just say, middle, top, end. An indicator as to where you squeeze the toothpaste tube . . . It is a wonderful ice-breaker.

Friendship is the thing that lasts within a marriage, and we must work on that friendship. Friendship and kindness to each other is the thing that endures into the sunset of latter years. I pray that you will be very close friends for the rest of your lives.

Traditions can vary a lot. Especially marrying into the military, where even telling the time is different. Being on time is drilled into the military so, as a wife, you will have to make sure you are ready at least five minutes before the scheduled time of departure. You might even set your watch five minutes fast. But, to the groom, a reminder that you cannot pull rank in marriage!

I have presided at many weddings; some where the couple read their own vows. I have never been to a wedding where the bride chose a reading that is also a vow. In choosing the passage from Ruth you are setting this marriage on a firm foundation – well done. Today you are not only taking wedding vows but you have taken it a step further in your soul betrothal in and through the words of Ruth. The book of Ruth combines all the traits of human life and character; Ruth is a book all can read with both pleasure and profit.

The Gospel of John proclaims Jesus informing us about love – that we are to love one another and remain in that love. Jesus tells us this so that our joy may be complete. The command of Jesus within this passage is that we must love each other as he has loved us.

You have both proclaimed your love for each other in a very powerful way. I know that your joy will be complete.

This recipe is a baseline for a newly married couple to log on to and to follow. Love must be sincere. Cling to what is good. Be devoted to one another. Honour one another above yourselves. Never be lacking in zeal, keep your spiritual fervour, serving the Lord. Be joyful in hope, patient in affliction, faithful in prayer. Share with God's people who are in need. Practise hospitality. Rejoice with those who rejoice; mourn with those who mourn. Live in harmony with one another. Be careful to do what is right in the eyes of everybody. If it is possible, as far as it depends on you, live at peace with everyone. Now that is the recipe for life.

I have found that drawing closer in relationship is rather like an equilateral triangle. God, husband on the left, wife on the right. The further away we move from each other, the further away from God we become; the closer we are to each other the closer to God we become. So strive to keep that triangle as small as possible, cleaving to each other . . . and to God. Be kind with each other, be creative within your marriage, and agree to disagree when you need to.

And remember that when you argue, hold hands. It is very difficult to argue when holding hands. I was at an Episcopal church some years ago, having offered that tip for 'good relationships' within my sermon. As people were leaving the church, in line, a wizened ninety-two-year-old came up to me and said in a very loud voice, 'My husband always said we should get naked when we argue.' I was most embarrassed, but we all had a good laugh. What a wonderful piece of advice. Perhaps you can both take a tip from that ninety-two-year-old – just be careful not to have a disagreement in the supermarket . . .

Jesus said, 'This is my command: love each other.' What a wonderful command this is . . . try to live this gospel for the rest of your lives. Enjoy your life, have fun, be kind to each other, enjoy each other. The 'like' is there, the 'love' is there, the 'friendship' is there; the recipe is complete, have a wonderful and blessed marriage with much fruit.

You have both invited God to the wedding. Make sure you invite God to the marriage. Listen again to the words of Jesus in John 15:12: 'My command is this: love each other as I have loved you.'

May God bless you both as one. In the name of God the Father, God the Son and God the Holy Spirit, Amen.

Nigel W.D. Mumford is an Episcopal priest and founder of 'By His Wounds Ministry', a ministry of Christian healing in the USA. Nigel was born in England and served for six years in Her Majesty's Royal Marine Commandos.

His conviction to pray for healing came in 1989 when his sister, Julie Sheldon, a ballet dancer with the Royal Ballet in London, was healed by God through the late Canon Jim Glennon. Nigel has three published books: *Hand to Hand: From Combat to Healing* (Church Publishing Inc.), *The Forgotten Touch* (Seabury Press) and *After the Trauma The Battle Begins: Post Trauma Healing* (Troy Bookmakers). Nigel lives with his wife Lynn in Virginia Beach, Virginia, USA. www.byhiswoundsministry.org.

16

WEDDING MESSAGE

Rich Nathan

In the Old Testament, we read about the wife of your youth, your companion, and your wife by covenant. These three terms refer to the three kinds of love that are essential for every good marriage.

The 'wife of your youth' refers to **romantic love**. It is what we talk about when we say two people are 'in love' with each other.

Your 'companion' refers to **friendship love**. In a great marriage, spouses will be each other's best friends.

Your 'wife by covenant' refers to **committed or covenant love** – love that is rooted in vows exchanged, committed love that stands by each other for better and for worse until death.

When we speak of romance, of course, we're speaking about intimacy and passion. We are also speaking about privacy and exclusivity. As you are marrying the wife of your youth, as you join together in passionate embrace, you are both building a secret history with each other – a history that no one else will share, a zone of seclusion that will be yours alone.

But a great marriage includes more than passion and romance. A great marriage also involves *friendship and companionship.* When you watch a really healthy marriage, you will see two people who really enjoy being with each other. They are best friends. They don't have to constantly fill the time with activity or diversions. Husbands and wives who are best friends don't get bored with each other, no matter how much time they spend together.

I love the fact that these two don't have to watch movies or spend a lot of money to enjoy being together. They find pleasure simply in talking and in being in one another's company. That is really healthy.

Friends have common interests. For this couple this begins with the priority they put on their relationship with the Lord. These are not two lukewarm Christians, or two people who are unevenly yoked. Anyone who knows these two, knows that they are passionate in their pursuit of God. I think that one of the things they find most attractive about each other is the fact that they each value Christ above everything else. They easily pray together. They have a joint spiritual life already. They love reading together and sharing the Bible with each other. And they are both so proud of each other's ministries and spiritual leadership. You should hear them brag about each other's gifts and each other's ministries! They are both Christian leaders in their own right.

But their commonness doesn't mean that they are two peas in a pod. These are not two identical people. Anyone who knows them immediately recognises that they are very different. They will never get bored because they are both very strong and tender people.

I asked them to write up a little description of what they love about each other. Here is what the groom wrote: 'What I love most about her is the strength and softness of her heart. This is a wonderfully unique combination that drew me to her. Her heart breaks with compassion for others and is so sweet and tender in relationship, yet it is not fragile. Her heart is strong and deeply grounded in God, and able to stand in the truth of who she is despite whatever may come. I love that she has a deeply personal and living relationship with Jesus. She listens to God on every issue of life, and actually expects him to speak. Her relationship with Jesus is not dependent on me or anyone else, but stands on its own. And so we now have the joy of joining together our spiritual lives in a very mutual way.'

Here is what the bride wrote: 'He has a *beautiful* heart. I love his heart so much. He is both strong and tender. I see his strength through the way he lives his life with integrity. He is committed to following Jesus wholeheartedly. And I see his tenderness in the way he cares for his family, his co-workers and, of course, me. He cares about my life and is a huge encouragement to me to live life fully!'

Strong and tender. Both of them used exactly the same words to describe each other. Yet their strength and tenderness come out in different ways. He is introspective, logical, deliberate and somewhat fussy. She is passionate. She has a fire inside. And she's no pushover.

Finally, *a great marriage is built on covenant*, the exchange of marriage vows before God and before those who love you both. Your marriage vows are the most solemn commitments you will ever make apart from your relationship with Christ. Nothing in life is more serious than your promise to take each other in plenty and in want, in joy and in sorrow, in sickness and in health, as long as you both shall live. You can change your citizenship. You can move to another country and God will not be offended. You can leave your jobs. You can quit virtually every other commitment. But the only human commitment that you are not permitted to quit or to leave is your marriage. You are swearing to God today that you are going to hang in there, regardless.

The Song of Solomon 8:6–7 says that love 'burns like a blazing fire, like a mighty flame. Many waters cannot quench love; rivers cannot sweep it away.' Water can quench any flame, but no force can quench covenant love.

It is inevitable that your love will be tested and tried by health problems, by financial problems, by ministry decisions, by challenges with your kids, and by life in general. But you can't quit. You may never give up on your marriage. You are making a covenant today with each other, with God and with everyone who is watching – your parents, your family and your friends. Covenant love, fuelled by the energy of God, will triumph over anything that life brings your way.

Rich Nathan has been serving as the first senior pastor of the Vineyard, Columbus, since 1987 (see www.vineyardcolumbus. org). Prior to pastoring, Rich taught Business Law at Ohio State University for five years. He has served on the National Board for Vineyard: A Community of Churches for over two decades. Rich is the author of *Who is My Enemy? Welcoming People the Church Rejects* (Zondervan, 2002) and co-authored *Empowered Evangelicals* (Ampelon, Revised 2009) with Ken Wilson. Rich was born and raised in New York City. He and his wife, Marlene, have been married for thirty-five years. They have two children and seven grandchildren.

17

TO LOVE AND TO CHERISH

Ed Olsworth-Peter

I've been to quite a few weddings, both as the one officiating and as a guest, and it's interesting that no two are ever the same even though there are very similar traditions and conventions. I've been to grand and lavish weddings and have been overwhelmed by the spectacle of the occasion, but likewise I've been to weddings with only a small number of people and been deeply moved by the intimacy of the service. At one of my previous churches they have a wedding album containing photographs from over five decades of weddings. You can certainly see obvious fashion trends documented over the years that make them similar but never the same.

One of the things that is the same are the words that the bride and groom say to one another, but again every wedding is different. Why? Because a marriage service is more than the words that are spoken, it's the meaning that they convey as an expression of the love between those two unique people.

There is a sentence in the marriage vows that always stands out to me: to love and to cherish. For me they sum up what marriage is about.

I'm sure most married people wouldn't dream of cheating on their spouse but it is ever so easy for subtle third loves to creep in. I'd hazard a guess that one of the most common is the act of iPad adultery. Imagine the scene: it's a Tuesday night and husband and wife have got in from work late and tired and decide to head up to bed at 9 p.m. Obviously, no self-respecting young professional couple would ever admit that publicly but we all know we do it. Once they've got their heads around the social disgrace of such an early bedtime, it dawns on them that this could actually be a nice opportunity to chat, catch up, snuggle and have some quality time together. Until, just as they are getting into bed, the iPad – seemingly minding its own business, just innocently hanging out, charging its battery next to the bed – beams its seductive smile from the bedside table. 'Hi there, you look like you need to unwind. Why not just finish that episode of *Grey's Anatomy* from the weekend?' it says in a slinky yet authoritative iPad kind of way, and you think, 'Well . . . I do kind of want to know how Dr Shepherd's 9 a.m. craniotomy turned out and if the musings of Meredith Grey will once again be the light-bulb moment of my week.' And before you know it you have committed iPad adultery while your irritated spouse pretends to be asleep but is really sulking on the other side of the bed.

We say, I love my husband or wife, and I love my iPad with the same word, but surely we don't mean the same thing? The English language is word poor when it comes to describing love whereas, in the Bible, Hebrew and Greek have many words for love.

The definition of love in 1 Corinthians 13 can help us. It tells us that love is patient, kind, rejoices in truth, is gentle, protects, trusts, hopes and perseveres (1 Corinthians 13:4–7) whereas it is not envious, boastful, proud, rude, self-seeking, easily angered, does not rejoice in evil and doesn't keep a record of wrongs. The first set of qualities reveals a selfless heart focused on the other person while the second describes a selfish attitude that is consumed with the self. It reminds us that love is more than what we say, and it's more than just warm feelings. It's about our attitude of heart and mind and how we live that out. For St Paul, writing to the Corinthian church, love was the glue that held one person to another and without this in a relationship our actions are meaningless. Maybe this is where cherishing comes in.

It's interesting that the word that follows the promise to 'love' in the marriage vows is the word to 'cherish'. To cherish your husband or wife is to take as much delight in their passions and victories as in your own and for them to take that same delight in you. I have a three-year-old niece. She's really into music. She's already a great singer and I love accompanying her on the piano to whatever toddler tune happens to be current. But the look on her face as she recites a new song, in perfect pitch, is priceless to her proud parents and always a moment to cherish.

For some reason the word cherish always reminds me of a cherry tree. If you've ever walked past a cherry tree when it's full with blossom, you'll know it grabs your attention. Now you can cherish a cherry tree in several ways: you can admire it from your kitchen window, you could even sit under it with a good book enjoying its shade, but to really cherish it you need to nurture, protect and even prune it at times. And the result is good fruit. Maybe it's not a coincidence that the fruit it produces comes in pairs? The act of cherishing is the outworking of the love within.

At the beginning of the service we heard the words: 'God is love. Whoever lives in love lives in God, and God in them' (1 John 4:16b). It's a reminder that love is a gift from God, and that his love is so embracing that it carries us and nurtures us. God, the greatest expression of love, is with you. And he didn't just tell us that he loved us but showed us in a real way by coming in human form to love the world by dying and rising again. The ultimate expression of loving and cherishing.

So, as you enter into married life, love and cherish one another surrounded and upheld by the love of your families and friends, and with the loving and cherishing nature and power of God himself.

Ed is a creative communicator and is interested in the active relationship between the arts, media and Christian faith. He has worked as a chaplain in two of London's West End theatres and is a council member of the Actors Church Union. He is currently vicar of two Anglican churches in south-east London, one exploring what it means to be an 'Urban Village' and the other developing the use of the creative arts to engage the wider community with its resident creative professionals. He is married to Lisa who is a professional performer and vocal coach. For more details, see www.holytrinitycentre.org.uk.

18

A CORD OF THREE STRANDS IS NOT QUICKLY BROKEN

Mary Pytches

Reading: Ecclesiastes 4:8–12

This passage is all about the benefits of a partnership between two people, of which marriage is one example.

1. The benefits of a marriage

Let's look at the benefits this couple are going to enjoy.

i. Fruitfulness: 'They have good return for their work.' Working together can be fun, but it is also more fruitful than working alone.

ii. Support: 'If one falls down the other can help them up.' We all need support and encouragement. Low self-esteem is so prevalent today that one of the greatest gifts we can offer one another is encouragement. Within all of us there are gifts and qualities just waiting to bud and bloom and they will do so, with a little encouragement.

iii. Warmth: 'If two lie down together they will keep warm.' It is a great benefit to have someone to warm one's feet on! But to me this also speaks of emotional warmth. Yes, we have physical needs, but we also have a great need to feel loved and appreciated. Those emotional needs will never be met 100 per cent by another person, but in a good marriage it can go a long way.

iv. Protection: 'Two are better than one because two can defend themselves.' Billy, aged four, said, 'When someone loves you, the way they say your name is different. You know that your name is safe in their mouth.' Fantastically astute for a four-year-old. Love protects; sometimes it feels as if the world is against you, but there is one person in the world who is for you.

So there are wonderful benefits in marriage but the blessings don't come on the cheap. A little *effort* is needed.

2. The cost of such a relationship?

'Marriage is like eating with chopsticks – it looks easy until you try it.'

i. Compromise: This is what I call 'blending and bending'. You come from different home backgrounds and bring your expectations, attitudes and ways of seeing life with you. It is your normality. It's the way you have always done it! Who is going to win? Well neither! You bend a little and then you find a way of blending both your backgrounds together. Together you form *your* home, *your way* **of doing things. That is what the first years are all about. And how is it accomplished? With . . .**

ii. Communication: When you first met and started going out, your mobile phone bills – or more than likely your parents' phone bills – were large. So now your bills may go down, but your communication must continue; in fact, it is even more important now. Good communication takes generosity and unselfishness. Marlene Dietrich said that it was the friends whom you could call up at 4 in the morning who counted. To listen to another's troubles at 4 in the morning takes a lot of patience! 'Friends are people who think about you when everybody else is thinking about themselves.' Communication also takes time and effort. It is easy to get it wrong. But without it how will we know what makes our partner tick? What their likes and dislikes are? It is easy to presume we know but not even those who have been married fifty years are mind readers. So communication is vital.

iii. Celebration: This hardly seems like a cost. But laughter and fun are what makes the world go round and are the things that oil the wheels of a good marriage. Celebrate your differences: that one of you is female, intuitive, laid back and travel sick while the other is male, tidy, organised and punctual. Celebrate even when there is nothing to celebrate. Chill out together. Have fun and, whatever happens, don't lose your sense of humour. It will often save the day.

iv. Commitment: Of course that is what today is all about. This couple are making a public commitment to each other. What are they committing to? The things I have mentioned, i.e. they are committing to working at *compromise, communication and celebration*. But it is also a commitment to love **and** faithfulness. Through thick and thin. It is going to be hard to make ends meet, so for a while it might be 'poorer rather than richer'. It is being faithful and loving one another through all the ups and downs of life.

But what is the secret to all this?

3. The secret of a good marriage

Ecclesiastes 4:12 – 'A cord of three strands is not quickly broken.' We have talked about 'blending', and how you now have to start blending your lives together. Two lives – two strands of the cord twisted together. But to have a really strong relationship you need the third strand.

None of us can afford to leave God out of our relationships. In the busyness of life it is easy to start compartmentalising God and only allowing him into certain parts. Jesus was a *guest* at the wedding in Cana of Galilee. He is a guest here – but he doesn't want to remain a guest. It is the presence of God which makes the difference.

- He gives us the grace to say those difficult words, 'I'm sorry' or 'I forgive you'.
- He gives us the power to keep changing and growing.
- He prods us when we are acting selfishly.
- It is his Spirit that produces in us the fruits of the Spirit – love, joy, peace, longsuffering and patience, which in the end will keep our marriages flourishing.

In a world increasingly hostile to marriage we must watch and pray lest we enter into temptation and leave God out.

Mary Pytches is married to Bishop David Pytches. She has four children and twelve grandchildren. She and David, with their four daughters, spent seventeen years in Chile as missionaries. When they returned to England in 1976 they went to St Andrew's, Chorleywood, staying there until they retired in 1996. Mary's major interest was developing a pastoral prayer ministry in the church. She has written books on subjects relating to personal growth. Although retired Mary still enjoys speaking and travelling.

19

THE NURSERY OF HEAVEN

Michael Rees

Reading: 1 Corinthians 13:1–13

Let me be the first to congratulate you both on your marriage. Well done! I speak not only for everyone here, but also for a few who unavoidably could not be with you today.

Who has had their hair done over the last day or two? I went to my barber yesterday. Now there was a barber who was churchwarden of a church that I know well in Cambridge. His name was Mr Taylor and he was a barber-surgeon, with his red-and-white-striped pole outside his shop: red for the surgeon part of his business and white for the shaving-soap side!

In 1613 he had a son called Jeremy. Later, Jeremy Taylor wrote two popular books called *Holy Living* and *Holy Dying*. In one of his books, he calls marriage 'the nursery of heaven'. For its children their nursery is a world all on its own. You two have committed yourselves to one another at your wedding. For you both your marriage is the nursery of heaven. Over the years many social and family pressures kept people together in marriage; this is not so true today, yet we still have high expectations of marriage.

First, marriage is a **loving relationship**, where each places the other above all else. It starts with mutual attraction, with shared hopes and assumptions.

Secondly, it's a **sexual relationship**. Physical attraction and shared satisfaction are realities we can't and shouldn't ignore.

Marriage is also a **biological relationship**, leading to the birth and bringing up of children. And it's a **social relationship**, as you both form a new family. It's made up, of course, of both your families, and also your friends – it's no longer his friends and her friends, but *our* friends. Friends, present and past, are important and need time to become part of your 'nursery'.

Marriage is also an **economic relationship**: your home, your possessions, your car and your incomes.

The nursery – a world of its own for you both. It gives time for the two of you to develop and mature in these relationships of your life together.

I'd like to share four mottos with you.

Pull together. During the last war captains of ships in convoy had two problems in the blackout: either drifting apart or crashing together. Both problems can occur in a marriage. From what I know of you both, you start with a common object, a common plan, which is to serve your joint Master, the Lord Jesus. Keep pulling together.

Plan together. As Christians you believe it was more than mere chance that brought you together. You believe that your Lord has a plan for you both. So it's not his or her plans but 'our plans'.

Play together. You have common friends. Continue to enjoy them. Have the same day off if it's at all possible. Have good holidays, although in the near future they may have to be a bit limited for obvious cash reasons! What about hobbies and interests? Shared hobbies can be part of your fun together.

Pray together. By this you acknowledge that there is a third dimension to your life. A dimension you have acknowledged because you've chosen to come to church today as you start your married life together. We are all three-dimensional people: first we have a material body; secondly a mind to think with; and thirdly a spirit which is the thing we love about other people. Prayer cultivates our spirits. So I would commend to you the practice of saying grace before meals. Have a time each day to pray together. Reading a passage from the Bible is a good way to start. It could be that you agree to have a time of quiet prayer, and then in turn one of you starts to pray the Lord's Prayer when they have finished. Or you could use written prayers together – there are many books of prayers published. Or again you could pray together using your own words to voice your hopes, your concerns and to bring before God the people for whom you pray. I would recommend a daily time cultivating that third dimension.

Pull together; plan together; play together; pray together. As we read in Amos 3:3, 'Do two walk together unless they have agreed to do so?'

Earlier in this service we heard your choice of a love poem. St Paul tells us that we may be great Christians, we may be good givers to those in need, we may have a great commitment to Jesus, but if we haven't got true love there's a big problem. May the Lord give you this kind of love for him, and for each other.

Love is a cup of tea in the early morning, ironing a shirt, sorting out a roof leak, booking a holiday, making sure the bills are paid and, of course, looking after your families – and much else besides. Ultimately these things will pass, but it is love that finally remains. Love is patient, love is kind, love never gives up, isn't selfish, isn't rude, isn't exasperated, is always hopeful; love keeps on to the end. The bad news is that these ideals are impossible to live up to.

Have you ever seen a biro stand on its point? That's impossible, just as impossible as making a marriage go on working over the years, caring for those around you, being an influence for Jesus Christ where he has put you. Let me show you – I put my biro on my book and it's standing on its point. 'Of course it's standing on its point,' you say. 'You're holding it!' You and I can't be Christian people unless the Lord Jesus holds us up and helps us. We can't live it in our own strength. The good news is that Jesus can hold you and give you his strength as you and I claim it day by day.

May the Lord bless you both as you set out as man and wife.

Michael Rees married Yoma in 1958, was ordained in 1959 and served in parishes for twenty-five years, the last being Holy Trinity Church, Cambridge. In 1984 he became Chief Secretary of Church Army serving 350 Evangelists in the UK linked to 900 worldwide. In 1990 he was appointed Canon Missioner in the Diocese of Chester, as well as being Vice-Dean of the Cathedral and County Ecumenical Officer. Since 2000 he has lived in retirement in King's Lynn, Norfolk. Their daughter Killy is married to J.John!

20

THE FIRES OF MARRIAGE

Rob Richards

Reading: 1 Corinthians 13:4–7

Today we witnessed a covenant made by you both within God's love. It is a covenant he will honour. Today is a wonderful step along that shared path.

Paul said, 'If I speak in the tongues of men or of angels, but do not have love, I am only a resounding gong or a clanging cymbal' (1 Corinthians 13:1). Hollywood tells us that love is a feeling. The Bible says that love is *practical*.

Marriage is a very high calling. There was a young bachelor lecturer at a theological college and he taught the students each year on 'Ten commandments for a stable marriage'. In time, he married and a year into his marriage he changed his title to 'Ten essential ingredients for a stable marriage'. After some years he amended the title further to 'Ten good ideas . . . ', then, finally, as he struggled with the high calling of being married, he plumped for 'Ten suggestions . . .'

God doesn't make suggestions. He calls us to love each other, in fact to love each other just as Jesus loves his church.

Be aware that you live in a culture of choice, a throwaway society. This gives us options which make commitment much more difficult. 'If it does not work then buy a new one.' Marriage is tarred with the same brush but marriage is not a contract that is there to be broken. So recognise that the culture of the day will work against you. It tries to see marriage as a *compromise*: 'I'll trade this if you trade that.' It is not a *compromise*. It is not *conditional*. It is a *covenant*. No strings attached, no small print, no catches. 'To have and to hold, from this day forward, for better for worse, for richer for poorer, in sickness and in health, 'til death do us part.' So we are here to encourage you in the commitment that you have both made.

Your rings are physical reminders of your vow and covenant. You are promising to love each other through thick and thin.

Like the lecturer at that theological college, I have some suggestions.

Marriage needs three fires to keep burning brightly:

1. The fire of friendship: Develop friendship such that you touch at every point of your lives. It's about companionship, being each other's soul-mate, being best friends. It means spending time together. Time together as best friends. You can test your friendship by the reading you chose: Love is patient and kind, love is not jealous, it does not boast, and it is not proud. Love is not rude, is not selfish and does not get upset with others; love does not count up wrongs that have been done. Love is not happy with evil but is happy with the truth. Love patiently accepts all things. It always trusts, always hopes, and always remains strong.

There are many things that can separate friends. Keep the fire of friendship burning.

2. The fire of physical love: As you join together in sexual union you become one flesh. It's a miracle that stands the test of a lifetime as you grow together. The Bible tells us it causes two individuals to become one new personality (Genesis 2:24).

We have a brand of glue called Unibond – one glue that holds all sorts of things together. Your promise today and God's gift to you both of physical love is like Unibond. God joins us in such a way that to divide us does not mean to separate us but requires each to be broken. You become *one flesh.* Keep the fires of physical love burning.

3. The fire of deep affection: 1 John 4:8 tells us that *God is love* and Jesus says, 'My command is this: love each other as I have loved you' (John 15:12). The Greek word is *agape*. This is growing, deep affection.

Marriage needs all three flames: friendship, physical union and deep affection.

But there is one other fire. It is the true source of all fire: the fire of God's love for you both. Nurture the love that never fails – God's love, as described in 1 Corinthians 13:4–7. There was only one person who loved like that. He laid down his life. 'Greater love has no one than this: to lay down one's life for one's friends' (John 15:13).

Jesus' love is patient and kind, is not jealous, does not boast, is not proud, is not rude, is not selfish and does not get upset with others; it does not count up wrongs that have been done, is not happy with evil but is happy with the truth, patiently accepts all things, always trusts, always hopes, and always remains strong.

God shows all these equalities in Jesus his Son. He opens wide his arms to embrace you both. It is in his name that you have made your promises. He will never fail you. Your marriage is like a triangle, with you both and God. In fact, marriage is a three-way relationship. Grow closer to God and you grow closer to each other. So allow his love like a fire to sustain the fires of your *friendship*, your *physical love* and your *deep affection.*

A good marriage must be created.
In the marriage the little things are the big things.
It is never being too old to hold hands.
It is remembering to say 'I love you' at least once a day.
It is never going to sleep angry.
It is having a mutual sense of values and common objectives.
It is standing together and facing the world . . .
It is forming a circle of love that gathers in the whole family.
It is speaking words of appreciation and demonstrating gratitude in thoughtful ways.
It is having the capacity to forgive and forget.
It is giving each other an atmosphere in which each can grow.
It is a common search for the good and the beautiful.
It is not only marrying the right person.
It is being the right partner.

Rob Richards is a former chaplain at Lee Abbey, previously associate vicar of St Andrew's, Chorleywood and since retirement has founded Connect, a ministry reflecting his passion: 'Through teaching and ministering in Word and Spirit and connecting the Body of Christ, we will together envision and equip the Church for the work of Ministry.' Married to Anna with a family of three, now all married, and seven grandchildren. For more information, see www.connectdorset.org.uk.

21

INTERTWINING TREES

John Ryeland

One of the most dramatic things I have seen at a wedding was when, on one occasion, the bride and groom had previously lit two candles and placed them on a table in the middle of the church. Standing in the middle was a larger unlit candle. After they had taken their vows, each of them took one of the candles and then they jointly lit the larger candle and proceeded to blow out their own candles. It was a powerful symbol of the two of them leaving behind something and starting something new together. Yet is that what this day really symbolises?

Another picture comes to mind which is far less dramatic and much messier, but perhaps it presents a truer picture of what marriage is really about.

The picture is of two trees planted next to each other. As they grow, the branches become intertwined, curling around each other, until in the end it is almost impossible to see which branch belongs to which tree. They are still separate but they have become one, and to seek to separate them would inevitably cause damage to the other. There are two reasons why this picture is so powerful on this particular day.

As you stand here as bride and groom, it is a picture of your future. You have already started to weave together but today represents a commitment by you both to allow someone else to influence your life, probably more than you can imagine. Perhaps each of you is tempted to think that you have a pretty shrewd idea of how you are going to influence and change the other and which particular branches of their life you want to replace with your own – but it probably doesn't work like that. The changes that marriage brings to our lives are mostly unplanned and unexpected and, if we saw them coming in advance, who knows what we would do!

Marriage is certainly a day of celebration, but it is also one of trust as you step into a new life of growth and influence.

The second reason why this picture of two intertwining trees is so powerful is that it also reminds us of something that marriage itself represents – namely the love between God and his people.

When the New Testament speaks about our relationship with Jesus, sometimes it uses the phrase of us being 'in Jesus' and sometimes it speaks about Jesus being 'in us'. At first it sounds impossible for both of these to be true at the same time, unless we go back to our picture of the interlocking trees. Who knows which tree is woven around the other – they are simply inseparable; to break one would be to hurt the other. For this reason marriage is such a beautiful picture of what Jesus came to bring us – although at some of the more challenging moments in our relationships that might seem a hard thing to remember!

The dream that Jesus puts in front of us all is a challenge to surrender or give ourselves to another so that together we will become far greater than we could ever be individually. This longing of Jesus applies to this couple beginning their life together here today but also gives hope to each one of us, that as we allow ourselves to be intertwined with God we will find the support, growth and comfort that we could not find in any other way.

John Ryeland is ordained in the Church of England and while working in various parishes he became particularly drawn to the healing ministry. In 1997 he became Director of The Christian Healing Mission (www.healingmission.org). As well as providing places where people can go for prayer, the Mission also has a teaching and training ministry in churches of all denominations. His particular focus is to encourage people to live with a real awareness of what it means to be loved by the Father and to sense the presence of Jesus with them in a tangible way. So often he has found that healing flows naturally from an encounter with Jesus. John is married to Gillian, who works at the Mission with him, and they have two adult daughters.

22

MARRIAGE ALWAYS

Tim Saiet

One of the greatest privileges I have, when taking a marriage service, is the opportunity to be the first to offer congratulations to the couple who have just got married. So I want to congratulate you both on your wedding today. Well done for your promises of love to one another. By being married before God today, you have made a commitment to live your lives God's way and that is a great decision to make.

Weddings are wonderful occasions. They are about new beginnings and new commitments. They are about love and happiness. They are about two people drawing together and getting to know one another, on a greater and more intimate level.

Not only do a man and a woman come together in marriage but they invite God to join them and to help them as they live a life together. Marriage is a way of life that we should honour and hold in high esteem. It should never be undertaken carelessly, lightly or selfishly. It needs to be undertaken respectfully, lovingly and responsibly; it should have been given serious thought. But when the decision is made there should be a time of celebration and congratulations and that is what today is all about. An acknowledgment of the love of two people for one another and the recognition that they have seriously thought about what a lifetime living together in love would mean and that they are choosing to willingly love one another whatever life brings them.

It is so easy to forget that we are all unique and different. It is also too easy to see the other's differences as something we would want to change. Marriage is not a relationship where we spend a life in trying to change the other, but where we allow ourselves to change, with love being the author of that change.

We all have a part today in the way that we shape our world and ourselves, and marriage is saying to others that we value and cherish commitment and love and friendship and intimacy. It is another way of saying that we will allow ourselves to grow and be shaped by marriage into more than we are today. Marriage has a way of shaping and transforming us.

Marriage is not about self but about being self-less. It is less about the self and more about the other . . . luckily we know we have someone who can help us on this journey. That someone is God. So there is another thing to celebrate today and that is the fact that you both believe in a marriage that is under God, that God has blessed your marriage, that God created marriage as part of his plan for his creation. It is exciting that you are willing to let God direct and lead you as you live your lives together.

Within marriage there are words that can hurt. Words like 'always'; we can use that word when we accuse our partner of behaviour that doesn't suit us. These are words that can harm and grieve love. Another word that can damage is 'never', as in 'You never do . . .' But we can turn some words around for good. We can use words to bring life and love to another person. So let's look at the word 'always'.

Always put the other first: That means involving each other in our decisions, so that we always share how we live our lives and the direction that we take. It is about sharing everything, including hopes and fears. It means that you own everything together and that all you have belongs to one another. You are both involved in all that you do and have.

A strong marriage is built by doing things for one another, always putting the other first. Always take time to listen to one another and to hear what each other says. Always talk and encourage each other. Always affirm and support each other. Always try to work together, sharing your vision for your lives. And finally always love one another and put the other person first.

Always invest in your love for one another: You should no longer say 'I' but 'we'. You should no longer say 'my' but 'our'. It is about sharing and spending time to grow with one another. Giving your lives in selfless love for one another is a gift that you can offer each other. The Bible tells us that 'Greater love has no one than this: to lay down one's life for one's friends' (John 15:13). Always invest in your love for one another. That also means investing in your friendship. The love that the Bible talks about is a love that looks outwards towards others and not inwards towards yourself. This is the love that God wants you to exhibit to each other; not a love that seeks your own ends but a love that gives to the other.

We are taught today to seek our own satisfaction before we seek the satisfaction of another but the Bible teaches the opposite: putting others first before we serve ourselves. If we seek the satisfaction of another then we find satisfaction. It is in serving that we find ourselves. It is in that action of serving one another that you will see your love grow and flourish.

Life is meant to be enjoyed. It is a gift from God. That means we are to have fun as well as work. Today we celebrate. Our lives can continue to be a celebration as you celebrate your love for God and for each other.

When we are grateful we find that gratitude fills us with hope and love. We are told in the Bible to give thanks at all times and in all places and there is something special about giving thanks for all we have in each other and for what God has done for us.

With these three ingredients and under the love of God, you can have a marriage made in heaven.

Tim Saiet is Vicar of St John the Evangelist Hildenborough. He is married to Charlotte and has three children. Tim is a former Royal Marine Commando and spent time coaching all types of skiing and outdoor winter pursuits. He has worked in the Arctic Circle and taught in several ski schools around the world. He spent much of his life as a professional illusionist and creative communicator. Tim previously spent three years as a church leader in London and three years as an evangelist with J.John.

23

UNITING DIVERSITY

David Shearman

In our 'brave modern world' communication has exploded and computers and compatibility are the language of the day. Information is everywhere. Millions are connected but what about the deeper reality of commitment and covenant?

The Christian understanding of marriage – which we celebrate in this service today – reveals marriage both as a covenant that God blesses and as a lifelong commitment which is a tangible expression of that covenant.

In the unique circumstances of this marriage we have a bride and groom whose native languages, continents of birth and cultures are very different. So the language we use to communicate starts with some challenges. Words are a great part of communication, and what shared language will the couple use? Beyond words, attitude, atmosphere and actions also communicate, either positively or negatively.

Gary Chapman wrote a great book entitled *The Five Love Languages* to encourage greater communication in our marriages. The five 'languages' he identified were:

Words of Affirmation: Learning the skill of unsolicited compliments, encouragement and the simple but powerful 'I love you'.

Quality Time: Learning how to be 'fully present' for each other, learning to listen and being attentive.

Gifts: More than the predictable and 'expected' – the thoughtful card, the unexpected flowers and surprises that add so much and speak so loud.

Acts of Service: Doing some of the 'boring' things: clearing up, laying tables, cups of tea, emptying the dishwasher and putting hot water bottles in the bed!

Physical Touch: The language of love in the bedroom will be so much clearer when the gentle touch, the holding of hands and lots of hugs and kisses are part of every day.

These foundational ingredients will help and strengthen your love life so that in every part of life you share a language that is *compatible* and *communicates*.

It all starts somewhere – perhaps with a look across a crowded room. I introduced myself to my wife-to-be nearly fifty years ago by sending her a birthday card – it wasn't very romantic but it did the trick! God did something much more outrageous and sublime:

'This is love: not that we loved God, but that he loved us and sent his Son as an atoning sacrifice for our sins' (1 John 4:10).

'God so loved the world that he gave his one and only Son' (John 3:16).

'Greater love has no one than this: to lay down one's life for one's friends . . . While we were still sinners, Christ died for us' (John 15:13; Romans 5:8).

This is the most powerful, explosive love ever seen on earth. It is his 'birthday card' to us. 'I want to know you, forgive you, love you and share in your life.'

As you have overcome and are still overcoming barriers that would limit your communication with each other, so God has overcome every barrier that would stop us receiving his love. With his love in each of your hearts you have a foundation for your love to become all that God intended it to be.

Every problem can be overcome. Every communication difficultly solved. With his love in your hearts fuelling your love for each other, the five love languages will blossom into a garden of beauty that others will want to observe.

So, as you begin a new life together, receive his love as the foundation of your love. What you build will last, what you grow will be fruitful, what you invest in will bring profit and all around you will understand that his love is the language of your love for each other.

David Shearman was Senior Minister of the Christian Centre Nottingham for thirty-five years before stepping down in September 2013. He still maintains a schedule of preaching and teaching worldwide (for details, see www.cathcon.org), has a heart to develop the next generation of leaders and is an Ecumenical Canon of Southwell Minster. He is married to Dorothy, and has two children and four grandchildren. Someone once described David as 'a Pentecostal monk, with tears'.

24

THE DANCE OF MARRIAGE

Roger Simpson

Reading: Ephesians 5:21–33

You have chosen as one of your readings a passage from Paul's letter to the Ephesians that was to completely change the character of marriage in the ancient world. It was radical and transforming then and it is radical and transforming today. It's what is needed in a society that is losing faith in marriage.

There are many pictures used to describe marriage. One of the ones that I love is that of the dance. Some marriages are like watching two people dancing together in harmony. Things are fine provided that both partners concentrate on their own steps. Problems come when you try to correct your partner's steps or do their steps for them. You usually end up in a heap on the floor! So what are the steps to dancing the dance of marriage together? Paul gives us two in this passage.

The first step: 'Husbands, love your wives, just as Christ loved the church.' This is a command. The word Paul uses for love is the little word *agape*. It's a Greek word that describes Jesus' self-sacrificial love for the church. It's stronger than the other Greek words for love: *fileo, eros, storge.* This type of love is not based on feelings.

It describes our behaviour. That's why Paul says husbands are to love their wives in the same way that Jesus Christ loves the church. He describes this love elsewhere as the sort of love that never gives up, cares more for others than for self, doesn't want what it doesn't have, isn't always 'me first', doesn't fly off the handle, puts up with anything, always looks for the best, never looks back and keeps going to the end. Wow! That's the sort of love that you are to give to your wife. That's the sort of love that Jesus Christ had for the church. That's to be our model. And it's not written just for you; it's for all of us here who are husbands.

The second step: 'Wives, submit yourselves to your own husbands as you do to the Lord.' Or, as *The Message* puts it, 'Wives, understand and support your husbands in ways that show your support for Christ.' What does this mean? Perhaps it's best to say what I think it *doesn't* mean. It doesn't mean being a doormat for your husband to walk all over. It is, to quote one woman writing about this passage, 'a voluntary, free, joyful and thankful partnership. It is supporting and encouraging your husband.' I remember one preacher saying that he thought Paul said husbands were to love their wives and wives were to submit to their husbands because that was what they each found most difficult! Husbands tend to love their work and wives often find it difficult to submit to their husbands because they are often better than them at doing things! Earlier on Paul writes, 'Submit to one another out of reverence for Christ.' We show our love by our submission.

Now I want to give you some practical hints for dancing the dance of marriage together in the years ahead. Firstly, keep Jesus Christ right in the centre of your marriage. Listen to his words: 'Are you tired? Worn out? Burned out on religion? Come to me. Get away with me and you'll recover your life . . . Walk with me and work with me – watch how I do it. Learn the unforced rhythms of grace . . . Keep company with me and you will learn to live freely and lightly' (Matthew 11:28–30, *The Message*). I love that! It expresses so clearly what it means to keep Jesus Christ right at the centre of your relationship. And as you do so you will find his life, love, power and forgiveness flowing through you both. So get away with him, learn from him, keep company with him. Watch what he does and you'll live freely and lightly.

Secondly, spice up your marriage. Somebody once said, 'Marriage is like a meal: without seasoning it is likely to be mediocre.' So how can you spice up your marriage? Sheldon Vanauken, a contemporary of C.S. Lewis at Oxford, uses a haunting phrase when talking about his own very happy marriage in his book, *A Severe Mercy*. 'A creeping separateness.' It's an issue in any marriage – how to stop that creeping separateness which inevitably leads to husbands and wives drifting apart? Tell each other regularly that you love each other. Learn to handle conflict. There will be conflict in every successful marriage. There's nothing wrong with conflict, it's how we handle it that matters. In the end it will succeed or fail on one little word: communication. So try and say, 'I feel . . .' rather than 'You always . . .' or 'You never . . .'

Keep talking together. Turn off the TV or get rid of it altogether. Talking is the greatest aphrodisiac. Roger Vann once said, 'For men good sex is important for a good relationship. For women a good relationship is a prerequisite for good sex.' He was absolutely right!

Do everything you can to live in harmony together. Don't let the sun go down on your anger. Talk things through. And if you get stuck on something, go and get some help. There's always someone there who will help you if you ask for it. And always affirm each other in public.

And finally, keep growing as individuals. You don't cease to be individuals when you're married. So keep growing. Make regular times where you can discuss together where things are at in your marriage. Grow with each other. You can anticipate the changes and grow together. So your wife may become a great motor mechanic and your husband may become a great gardener. Above all, put the other one first. Respect each other's individuality.

So as you take this great step together our prayers and our love are with you. As you learn to dance the dance of marriage together remember that you have Jesus Christ there beside you at all times.

Roger Simpson was Vicar of St Michael Le Belfrey, York for eleven years and in June 2010 was appointed as Associate Minister and Evangelist to the North by the Archbishop of York. Roger is passionate about spreading the gospel of Jesus, and works with teams throughout the north of England doing just this in parishes, universities, pubs and clubs, streets and schools. He is married to Ursula who is Priest in Charge of St Barnabas, Leeman Road, and they have five grown-up children who are all married; they became proud grandparents for the first time in October 2012. Roger enjoys watercolour painting and playing golf, and he once appeared on page 3 of the *Sun*!

25

FIGHTING FOR MARRIAGE

Jill Sweetman

We are so happy when the wedding day comes! We think, 'Finally, it's here. I've made it. No more struggles.' These thoughts, though, are not true. Marriage is a beginning. A couple is doing life together, and life can sometimes get in the way. Marriage is a battlefield at a whole new level.

We can all too often think that the battle is in the dating scene. We purposefully pursue the person we want, relentlessly, finding things they like and trying to get involved in those areas so we can be more attractive to them. Then, when the vows are made, we stop! The connection is no longer there. Where are the romance and the companionship? If it was forged on false expectations, it fizzles and fades. Do not fear, newlyweds, marriage is not doomed to failure, but it is also not as easy as it looks. In the twenty-eight years that I have been married to Dean, I have found several factors that help to build strong marriages. The first is to determine that our marriage will be our one and only. We will not even consider the 'get out of marriage free card' that society presents through easy divorce. We will hold true to our vows despite our doubts and fears. If there is struggle, we will commit to work through it, even if that means that we ask for help.

The second factor is that we, together, are willing to fight! The vow is 'for better or for worse'. Are we ready to face both? This willingness is better known as commitment. Commitment in a relationship is so important! It means that we will resist temptation. Paul, in 2 Timothy 2:22, instructs us to flee the desires of youth. There will be things that we used to do, used to love and used to want that will have no place in the marriage. For example, looking at someone whom you find very attractive but who is not your spouse. No matter our age, married or single, desire for others is real. It does not disappear just because we are having sex on a regular basis. Sexual desire might diminish over the years, but the mind can stay active. We must decide daily to walk away from situations that could damage our marriage, take steps to not take our spouses for granted, and make the enhancement of our marriage the main goal.

The Bible teaches us to choose our thoughts carefully. This is the third factor: thought life. Do we indulge in our fantasies or do we dwell on what is true, noble, right, pure, lovely, excellent or praiseworthy? We can learn to discipline our minds. All sinful actions begin as a thought. Paul instructs us in Romans 12:2 about renewing the mind. A great gauge to use in measuring thoughts is this: will my spouse like what I am thinking right now? If the answer is 'no', cast that thought to God and move on. The renewing of our thought life is a daily battle but, with God, we can be victorious.

Thoughts are connected to the fourth factor: how we talk about our spouses when they are not around. Our personal portrayal of our spouses is on a par with how we think about them. The media all too often portrays women sitting around a table complaining about their idiotic husbands. This is so damaging! Our words have power, so we need to refrain from negative talk and criticisms about our spouse to others, particularly to those of the opposite sex. We are human. We need a sympathetic ear from time to time, but this ear should be attached to a trusted friend who can give sound advice after we are done lamenting. Marital complaint should never be the topic of a girls' or a guys' night out. Our spouse will have faults, but we grow and mature to look beyond those to the traits that drew us to our spouse in the first place.

Factor five is being honest. Being honest about marriage is just as important as committing to make it work. If there is an issue neither of us can work out, we need to seek help. Secrets, too, are a bad idea in marriage, as we can feel cheated if and when we find out that our spouse has kept a secret from us. Secrets create problems, so open communication is key. It is also invaluable to have a network of trusted friends who have insight into our lives and can give an honest assessment when we cannot.

Factor six is trust. Marriage is strengthened by our trust in one another. We keep our spouse's most intimate secrets as they keep ours. Set limits to protect that trust and talk it through. Agree upon them. Hold each other accountable to them. Put specific restrictions on spousal interaction with the opposite sex. These boundaries can seem extreme but they are necessary in helping each other avoid tempting situations.

The seventh and most important factor is church. The community built within a church should be one of acceptance and love. It is here that we can find those close, trusted friends who aid us in keeping our lives together. They help us deal with guilt perhaps born from keeping secrets or in addressing an aspect of our attitude that is unknowingly causing damage to our marriage. A good church provides biblical teaching and guidance for a marriage.

No marriage is without problems; however, if we focus on our commitment and remember that marriage is a daily battle, we set ourselves up for success. Marriage is a sacred trust created by God for us. Let's do it well.

Jill Sweetman and her husband Dean are a part of the C3 Church based in Australia. In 1996, Dean and Jill moved from Sydney, Australia, to Lawrenceville, Georgia, USA to plant a church. They now oversee thirty thriving C3 churches across both North and South America. Jill is a sought-after expert in the fields of marriage, family and relationships. Jill has authored, *Marriage: How to Remain Married Forever* and *Little Shakers: Parenting in the 21st Century*. Jill has two grown-up sons and two amazing daughters-in-law. You can check out more on Jill's blog: jillsweetman.com. You can also follow her on twitter: @jillsweetman

26

PUT ON LOVE

Ruth Turner

Reading: Colossians 3:12–20

May I be the first to congratulate you – well done you! It is a brave thing you have done to commit to each other publicly.

As you start out in married life, lots of people will give you their pieces of advice; however, there is no better guidance than that which is found in the Bible reading you have chosen for today.

This passage in Colossians is all about 'putting on'. By that I mean, just as we put on our glad rags for today's ceremony (and very smart you all look too) so we need to put on spiritual clothes.

What does he say to put on? Compassion, kindness, humility, gentleness, patience and being quick to forgive; and as if that wasn't more than enough he then says to put on love. No problem. And it *sounds* easy until you actually have to do it. But what does 'putting on love' actually look like?

As human beings the thing we fear most is being vulnerable, being exposed; the thing we desire most is connection.

Ironically and unfortunately, the way to real connection is through being vulnerable – enabling the other to see who we really are.

Each of us has a fence of protection around us, to stop people coming too close and hurting us. You only have to have someone invade your personal space as they talk to you to be able to imagine it. When we fall in love, that fence comes down and we allow the other person to come right up close and we are happy to be vulnerable. On average, two years later our protective fence goes back up and it is at *that* point where love really begins; that is when we choose to commit to the other, to love. Putting on love is a choice not a feeling.

It is interesting to look at the journey these two people have made from first meeting to being married. Think of all the little things that pushed their relationship towards commitment rather than walking away, risking vulnerability rather than safety.

I don't know what you think about God, but he is described as love. God *is* love. Love is the very essence of who he is; he can't help himself, he just is – love. He wants a relationship with each one of us and has made the first move by becoming very vulnerable. Jesus, God's Son, became a human being; he took on flesh, the Bible says, to show us what God was like, to show us how much he loved us. God became human – how incredibly risky! – did he not know how fragile humans are? I mean, he might have got sick or been killed for goodness' sake!

A friend of mine said to his wife recently, 'I took a risk marrying you but not nearly as big a risk as you did marrying me!' It's true – it is a step of faith.

Put on love. The risk is that we make ourselves vulnerable but then have no connection.

I heard of a couple who were having such problems that they started seeing a counsellor. After a few weeks of just listening to them the counsellor got up and asked the wife to stand. Then he gave her the most enormous bear-hug. He said to the husband, 'She needs that at least twice a week.' The husband was quiet for a bit then nodded and said, 'Well, I can bring her in on Tuesdays and Fridays'!

Marriage is a risk; it is about choosing to be vulnerable, choosing to put on love, but it is also most rewarding if both husband *and* wife choose to put on love. Then we get the connection we crave and receive love from each other.

God, the Lord of the universe, wants a connection with us. For many of us it seems incredibly risky and makes us seem too vulnerable; but remember that God made himself vulnerable first and continues to be committed to us wholeheartedly, hoping that we will respond to his keenness and risk our hearts to him.

So please continue to choose to put on love, not only in your journey together but also in your relationship with God in your journey of faith. It's risky to live out of a place of vulnerability, but so, so rewarding. Hang on to that in the rollercoaster ride ahead.

Ruth Turner trained as a musician and music teacher then worked as a music director/worship leader for many years: in Wollongong, Australia; at St Aldate's Church, Oxford (ten years) and St Alkmund's Church in Derby. Ruth was ordained in 2009 and is now Team Vicar of St Andrew's Community Church (LEP) in Dronfield Woodhouse, near Sheffield.

27

THE CHIEF END OF MARRIAGE

Simon Vibert

Reading: Ephesians 5:21–33

The battle of the sexes:

> Any husband who says, 'My wife and I are completely equal partners,' is talking about either a law firm or a hand of bridge.
> *Bill Cosby*

> Keep your eyes wide open before marriage, half shut afterwards.
> *Benjamin Franklin*

> My wife dresses to kill.
> She cooks the same way.
> *Henry Youngman*

> My wife and I were happy for twenty years. Then we met.
> *Rodney Dangerfield*

> A husband said to his wife, 'No, I don't hate your relatives. In fact, I like your mother-in-law better than I like mine.'

The changing relationship between men and women must be the most remarkable of all the social revolutions of the last hundred years. Before then, role relationships were fairly straightforward. The best education was given to the male in the household. He it was who went out to earn a living. Women stayed at home, kept the house in order and reared the children.

Many things have changed. Women's capability has proved to be equal to men's. They have equal choice in education and all other opportunities. We have had a female Prime Minister and female clergy and corporate executives. Contraception has enabled women to make planned choices about when/whether to have children and how many to have. Cultural attitudes have changed and old prejudices about what is 'no job for a woman' seem to be rules made to be broken!

The popular argument says that the apostle Paul's understanding of the role of women was determined by the patriarchal culture in which he lived. In that culture women were subordinate, poorly educated and tied to the home. Consequently, it is sometimes assumed, Paul's teaching on role-relationships is no longer relevant.

However, the difficultly is that Paul does *not* base his understanding of the role-relationships of men and women on the basis of the prevailing *culture* – but rather upon *creation*. Indeed, the reasons why men and women are made this way go behind even creation and stem from the relationship between God the Father and the Son. Having said that, let's come to see what the passage before us actually says. Let's first look at the husband's role.

Husbands, how are you to relate to your wives? (v.25)

To love as Christ loved the church (v.25). How did Christ do that? By giving up everything for her (v.2). Not just the cheque book, etc., but *himself*. Most husbands are better at giving things than themselves. First, then, is *sacrificial giving.*

To love as he loves his own body (v.29). A husband is called to love even as we love our own bodies; to give his all for his wife. The second picture is that of *intimate caring.*

How, then, wives, are you to love your husbands? (v.22)

By submitting. This is only possible if the wife submits because *behind* the husband she sees Christ. This idea of *headship* is the sticking point for many people. But notice that there is a distinction between the *obedience* required of children (6:1) and the *submission* required of wives. The passage does not say 'husbands make your wives submit' nor 'wives make your husbands love you'. No – both are called upon to look out for *each other's* rights. However, this is still very unpopular teaching today. And the reason we are so uncomfortable with it is because of our fallen natures. The principle of headship was there in the original creation (1 Corinthians 11). But notice what happened after the rebellion in the garden (Genesis 3:15–19): headship became rule and work became toil. Taking work as an example, we say we hate work, but we can't live without it – we are made for work. Yet it is a slog, i.e. that which is good – work – has become twisted by our fallen natures. So, too, with the principle of headship. I don't know of many wives who would not willingly submit to a husband who loved them as Christ loved the church.

And yet Ephesians 5 surely hints at what we see manifested all the time today: the wife will seek to wear the trousers in the marriage and yet will not be happy in that role because she wants a husband to give a godly lead. And the husband is guilty of abdicating that responsibility to lead and actually never fully gives himself up for his wife: he retains his old drinking mates; goes off to do his hobbies on his own; never opens up his heart to his wife; grunts from behind the paper; doesn't instruct the children.

You see, in the last thirty years we have said: that men and women are equal; that equal worth means equal opportunity and equal rights; and that equal rights means equal roles. And though there was some pretty mucky bathwater there, I fear that we threw out the baby at some point. For never before has there been so much confusion between men's and women's roles as today. The wife feels guilty for staying at home caring for the children; the husband feels stretched being the caring modern man.

Ephesians 5 teaches us that we need to be in a caring partnership – of loving *and* submission – each looking out for the other person's rights.

Conclusion (v.32)

God didn't just look around creation and think, 'Hmmm, how can I give a good example of my loving relationship with the church?' Rather, marriage is given as an enacted parable – for all the world to see – of how God relates to humanity. Therefore, when we love and submit as God has taught us, husbands witness to the kind of love which Christ has for the church and wives witness to the kind of love the church should show to Christ.

We won't be able to put these principles into practice until we see our marriage as a three-way partnership: behind the wife, the husband is to see Christ as the sacrificial lover; and behind the husband, the wife is to see the church submitting to Christ.

Simon Vibert is Vice Principal of Wycliffe Hall in Oxford. He has significant interest in theological training overseas, particularly in Tanzania, Zambia, Serbia and Haiti. He has eighteen years' experience in parish ministry. The last eight years were as Vicar of St Luke's Church, Wimbledon Park. He has written in the areas of human sexuality and contemporary culture and preaching: *Excellence in Preaching: Learning from the Best* (IVP, 2011). Simon is married to Caroline and they have three children and one grandchild.

ALSO BY J.JOHN

Proclaiming Christmas

Our churches are never better attended than during the Christmas season. This gives a special opportunity to deliver a message to our congregations, to present God Incarnate and to creatively preach the 'original script'.

J.John asked friends, all known for their gift as creative communicators, for their best Christmas sermon, and the result is this book. This will not only enlighten, encourage and inspire you as you read it, but will inform and equip all preachers with ideas and content.

Also, this is for anyone who likes reading sermons (like J.John!) to give you a faith-lift.

To order please visit:
www.philotrust.com